ENGLISH Alive

Level 5

Teacher's Resource Book

Barry Scholes and Gill Atha

Collins Educational

ISBN 000314 335-X
© Collins Educational 1991.
All rights reserved.

Collins Educational

Contents

	Page
Introduction to the *English Alive* course	4
Outline of the course	4
Aims	5

Level 5

Introduction	5
Contents of Book 5	6
Teacher's Notes and Activity Masters	7
Assessment Masters — test papers	108

Appendices

Pupil Profile (National Curriculum)	112
Adventures in English skills chart	114
Contents of Level 5 Listening Skills cassette	115
Answer cards for Listening Skills masters	116
Adventures in English — outline of series	120
Outline of *Wreckers' Rock* and *McGinty's Gold*	120
Wreckers' Rock pupil's record sheet (National Curriculum)	123
McGinty's Gold pupil's record sheet (National Curriculum)	124
Index	125
National Curriculum Attainment Targets: Level 5	132

Introduction

Outline of the course:

National Curriculum	Key Stage One				Key Stage Two		
	Level 1	Level 2	Level 3		Level 4		Level 5
English Alive	Starter	Approach	Level 1	Level 2	Level 3	Level 4	Level 5
Adventures in English Software		Goblin Winter	Spooky Tower	Spell Bound	Pirate's Treasure	Wreckers' Rock	McGinty's Gold

	National Curriculum							
	Level 1	Level 2		Level 3		Level 4		Level 5
English Alive	Starter	Starter	Approach	Level 1	Level 2	Level 3	Level 4	Level 5
AT1 Speaking/ Listening	a,b,c,	a,b,c,d,e	a,b,c,d,e	a,b,c,d	a,b,c,d	a,b,c,d	a,b,c,d	a,b,c,d,e
AT2 Reading	b,d	b,c,d,e	a,b,c,d,e,f	a,c,d,e,f	a,b,c,d,e,f	a,b,c,d	a,b,c,d	a,b,c,d,e
AT3 Writing	a	a,b,c	a,b,c,d	a,b,c,d,e	a,b,c,d,e	a,b,c,d,e	a,b,c,d,e	a,b,c,d,e
AT4 Spelling	a,b,	d	b,d	a,b,d	a,b,c,d	a		a
AT5 Handwriting	a			a	a			
AT4/5 Presentation								a,b,

Level	Age	Pupil's Book	Listening Skills Cassettes	Computer Software (Adventures in English)
Starter	5+	{ Starter Masters { Starter Workbooks	Starter Cassette "	———
Approach	6-7	Approach Book	Approach cassette	Goblin Winter
Level 1	7-8	Book 1	Level 1 Cassette	Spooky Towers
Level 2	8-9	Book 2	Level 2 cassette	Spellbound
Level 3	9-10	Book 3	Level 3 cassette	Pirate's Treasure
Level 4	10-11	Book 4	Level 4 cassette	Wreckers' Rock
Level 5	11-12	Book 5	Level 5 cassette	McGinty's Gold

English Alive is a complete Primary English course in seven levels, covering the age range 5+ to 12+. It has been designed with full regard to the National Curriculum and the recommendations of the Bullock and Kingman Reports. It is carefully and systematically structured to develop the full range of English skills: speaking, listening, reading and writing and the study of language.

These skills are developed within the context of carefully chosen themes which link language development with other areas of the curriculum and offer wide scope for a variety of follow-up work. The literary extracts which provide the stimuli for many of these themes have been selected to extend the experience of the children.

The course begins in the Infant Department with photocopiable Starter sheets, and three Starter Workbooks. An

Approach Book of fourteen units then leads on to the main part of the programme in Levels 1-5.

Each level is supported by the *Teacher's Resource Book* which contains a wealth of follow-up work in the form of photocopiable masters and ideas for the teacher to develop. There is also an audio cassette which provides a structured approach to the development of listening skills. Each tape links with photocopiable masters in the Resource Book.

Also available is the *Adventures in English* series of computer programs. Each adventure links with one of the books and is accompanied by Pressure-fax Spiritmaster activity sheets which provide a variety of stimulating follow-up work.

Aims of the course:

The course aims to provide **the children** with opportunities to:

- widen ability and experience in reading, writing, listening and speaking.
- link the work done in English to work covered in other disciplines so that the learning that takes place is relevant and meaningful.
- foster in themselves an appreciation and enjoyment of many kinds of literature:— stories, prose (factual and fiction), plays, poems etc.
- examine and interpret a wide range of stimuli (familiar and new) — literary, visual and aural — and to react in a variety of ways to these stimuli i.e. through written work, debate, drama etc.
- work individually and in groups on a variety of projects (written and oral) as stimulated by this wide range of stimuli.
- gain increasing clarity in oral and written expression, both factual and creative.
- gain an increased sense of oral and written language for different purposes.

The course aims to provide **the teacher** with:

- A pupil profile to record pupil's work, progress and mastery of skills. The profile is cross referenced to the attainment targets of the National Curriculum of England and Wales.
- sheets to record individual pupils' work, progress and mastery of skills

- a complete and balanced language course which develops the whole range of language skills and is firmly based on the National Curriculum and the recommendations of the Bullock and Kingman Reports.
- a thematic approach to language teaching which is organised to link with other areas of the curriculum; reinforcing the work and giving it meaning and purpose.
- a thorough, colourful and attractive way of presenting children with a variety of resources — literary, visual and aural — to stimulate and encourage their knowledge and appreciation of the language, its structure and how it can be used most effectively.

Level 5

The material in Book 5 is organised into six thematic units.

Unit structure

The stimuli for each unit are extracts from children's books, poems, or factual material in a variety of forms.

The poems and extracts have been selected with regard to their quality, the thoughts and feelings of the writers, and their appeal to children. A wide variety of writing styles and subject matter is represented. The comprehensive range of factual material is designed to help in the development of study skills, logical deduction and judgement. Such skills will link to other subjects across the curriculum.

Each unit is completed by activities to develop language and writing skills.

Notes and Masters

The teacher's notes and photocopiable masters in this Resource Book are intended to complement and extend each unit. They are grouped together, unit by unit, for easy reference.

It is left to the discretion of the teacher which of the masters is appropriate to any child or group. Some of the masters have been designed to give further practice material for the slow learner; others extend the language skills and are appropriate to the more able child. Our aim has been to provide a variety of masters to suit the ability range found in most classrooms.

Certain masters have been designated Skillmasters. Each Skillmaster provides clear explanations and graded practice for a specific skill. It may be kept by the pupil as a permanent reference sheet. Skillmasters are especially useful where a child has a specific difficulty, and those from earlier levels will be helpful where revision practice is required.

Also included are specially written group prediction stories, and Assessment Masters for use at the end of Book 5 to test progress. In addition to the masters there are suggestions for the development of speaking skills, and a range of follow-up work to link language skills to the rest of the curriculum.

Level 5 Listening Skills Cassette

Each level of *English Alive* has a Listening Skills cassette which together with the associated activity sheets provides for a carefully structured development of listening skills.

All instructions for the children are recorded on the tape to allow them to work independently. Photocopiable masters which can be made into pupils' self-marking answer cards appear in the Appendices, together with a full contents list for the cassette.

Pupil Profile

English Alive is cross-referenced to the National Curriculum of England and Wales, and the attainment target for each activity is clearly identified throughout the Resource Books: e.g. AT3/5b refers to Attainment Target 3, Level 5 (b). The pupil's work, progress and mastery of these skills may be recorded using the Pupil Profile found on page 112. Any method of recording may be used: e.g. shading, ticking, ringing, etc. Mastery of a particular attainment target may be indicated by an appropriate marking of the attainment target heading.

Level 5 Book: Contents

Unit	Title	Page
1	Living Together	2
2	Journeys	18
3	The Media	34
4	The "Titanic"	58
5	Changes	68
6	A Better World?	84

Level 5 Masters: Contents

UNIT 1
5.1a Group prediction: *The Emerald Necklace* — 1 **AT1/5b; AT2/5b**
5.1b Group prediction: *The Emerald Necklace* — 2 **AT1/5b; AT2/5b**
5.1c Group prediction: *The Emerald Necklace* — 3 **AT1/5b; AT2/5b**
5.1d Group prediction: *The Emerald Necklace* — 4 **AT1/5b; AT2/5b**
5.1e Skillmaster: comparison of adjectives — 1 **AT4/5a; ATs1-4**
5.1f Skillmaster: comparison of adjectives — 2 **AT4/5a; ATs1-4**
5.1g Skillmaster: letter writing **AT3/5a**
5.1h Compound words **AT4/5a; AT2/5d**
5.1i Fact find: People and Places **AT2/5d**
5.1j Listening skills: main idea/cause and effect **AT2/5b**
5.1k Listening skills: finding evidence **AT2/5b**
5.1l Listening skills: detail/recognition of same idea in different words **AT2/5b**

UNIT 2
5.2a Letter writing/railway timetable **AT2/5d; AT3/5a**
5.2b Giving directions: street plan **AT2/5d; AT3/5a**
5.2c Amberhurst Village: adding details to a map (Links to page 21 of pupil's book) **AT2/5d**
5.2d Treasure Hunt: context clues/use of maps **AT2/5d**
5.2e People and Their Countries: use of reference library **AT2/5d**
5.2f Holiday Booking Form (Links to page 31 of pupil's book) **AT2/5d; AT3/5a**
5.2g World Traveller: using reference material **AT2/5d**
5.2h Sorting **AT2/5d**
5.2i Word study: The Story of Our Language (Links to pages 22-3 of pupil's book) **AT2/5d**
5.2j Prefixes: *con-, en-, for-, sub-* **AT4/5a**
5.2k Skillmaster: simple past tense with helping verb **ATs1-4**
5.2l Listening skills: aural memory — recall of detail **AT2/5b**
5.2m Listening skills: points of view/fact and opinion **AT2/5b-c**

UNIT 3
5.3a Group prediction: *Fugitive* — 1 **AT1/5b; AT2/5b**
5.3b Group prediction: *Fugitive* — 2 **AT1/5b; AT2/5b**
5.3c Group prediction: *Fugitive* — 3 **AT1/5b; AT2/5b**

5.3d Group prediction: *Fugitive* — 4
AT1/5b; AT2/5b

5.3e Modelling: hierarchies   AT3/5a

5.3f Skillmaster: search reading   AT2/5d

5.3g Skillmaster: direct and reported speech — 1   AT3/5a

5.3h Skillmaster: direct and reported speech — 2   AT3/5a

5.3i Close examination of text: *The Daily Record*   AT2/5b-c

5.3j Close examination of text: *The Wessex Observer*   AT2/5b-c

5.3k News Editor — 1: news items

5.3l News Editor — 2: news items

5.3m Listening skills: News Room — 1: selection/main idea   AT3/5a

5.3n Listening skills: News room — 2: listening for detail/making notes   AT3/5a

5.3o Designing packaging/creating an advertisement   AT3/5a

5.3p Advertisement evaluation sheet   AT2/5b-c; AT3/5a

5.3q Story Board: TV advertisement/ programme planning sheet   AT2/5a

5.3r Recipes for biscuit bases   AT2/5d

5.3s Recipes for fillings and toppings   AT2/5d

5.3t Packaging suggestions   AT2/5d

5.3u Listening skills: following arguments/selecting suitable music for an advertisement   AT2/5a-b; AT3/5c-e

UNIT 4

5.4a Modelling: time line   AT3/5a

5.4b Cloze procedure   AT2/5b

5.4c Fact find: Famous Ships   AT2/5d

5.4d Fact find: Picture Search   AT2/5d

5.4e Reference skills/writing   AT2/5d; AT3/5a-d

5.4f Nautical word search   ATs1-4

5.4g Listening skills: from *A Night to Remember*: selection — listening for specific detail   AT2/5d; AT3/5a-d

UNIT 5

5.5a Modelling: graphs   AT3/5a

5.5b Listening skills: evaluating a speaker's attitude   AT2/5b-c

5.5c Fact find: encyclopedia   AT2/5d

5.5d Fact find: Guinness Book of Records   AT2/5d

5.5e Americanisms   ATs1-4

5.5f Prefixes   AT4/5a; ATs1-4

5.5g Skillmaster: future tense   ATs1-4

5.5h Group prediction: *Justice* — 1
AT1/5b; AT2/5b

5.5i Group prediction: *Justice* — 2
AT1/5b; AT2/5b

5.5j Group prediction: *Justice* — 3
AT1/5b; AT2/5b

5.5k Group prediction: *Justice* — 4
AT1/5b; AT2/5b

5.5l Listening skills: evaluating a speaker's attitude   AT1/5b; AT2/5b

UNIT 6

5.6a Re-cycling paper: following instructions   AT2/5d

5.6b Making papier mache: modelling — picture strips   AT2/5d; AT3/5a

5.6c Listening skills: following an argument/persuasion/pressure/ emotionally charged words   AT1/5b; AT2/5b; AT2/5d; AT3/5a-e

5.6d Group prediction: *Aliens* — 1
AT1/5b; AT2/5b

5.6e Group prediction: *Aliens* — 2
AT1/5b; AT2/5b

5.6f Group prediction: *Aliens* — 3
AT1/5b; AT2/5b

5.6g Group prediction: *Aliens* — 4
AT1/5b; AT2/5b

5.6h Assessment Master: writing skills   AT3/5a-e

5.6i Assessment Master: reading skills — 1   AT2/5b

5.6j Assessment Master: reading skills — 2   AT2/5b & d

5.6k Assessment Master: assignment   AT1/5d; AT3/5a & d

Unit 1

Theme — Living Together
Stimuli — from *My Mate Shofiq* by Jan Needle, Andre Deutsch
'I've Got an Apple Ready' & 'The Bully Asleep' by John Walsh from *The Roundabout by the Sea*, OUP
Listening cassette: *The Runaway Summer* by Nina Bawden, Victor Gollancz

AT1   Speaking/listening
5a   reporting on past and present experiences
5b   reasoning
5b   speculation
5b   view points changing with age
5b & d   video recording the group's different opinions:
— evaluation of the recording

— making an improved version
— re-assessing results

ATs1-4 Word study
* definitions
* idioms
* expressing the same idea in different words

AT2 Reading
"My Mate Shofiq":
5b — speculation
5b — inference
5b — evaluation
5d — sequencing events
5e — author's choice of words

"I've Got an Apply Ready" & "The Bully Asleep":
5a — comparison of the poems
5b — appreciation
5b — inference
5b — imaginative response
5b — speculation
5e — poet's choice of words
5d Venn diagrams
5c-d opinion poll: reading for detail
5c differences of opinion:
— evaluation
— persuasion
5c picture stimulus for points of view examination

AT3 Writing
Expressive:
5a-e narrative prose, writer as participant
Poetic:
5a & d list poem — "Friendship"
5a-e narrative prose, writer as spectator
5a-e dialogue for drama
Transactional:
5a setting out an envelope
5a recording information (annotated list)
5a Venn diagrams:
— recording information
— making up questions about diagram
5a-e recording events in passages
5a-e letter to a pen pal
5a-e letter expressing opinion
5a-e replying to letters

AT4/5 Presentation
5a root words, prefixes and suffixes

Activity sheets:
5.1a group prediction: *The Emerald Necklace* — 1 **AT1/5b; AT2/5b**
5.1b group prediction: *The Emerald Necklace* — 2 **AT1/5b; AT2/5b**
5.1c group prediction: *The Emerald Necklace* — 3 **AT1/5b; AT2/5b**
5.1d group prediction: *The Emerald Necklace* — 4 **AT1/5b; AT2/5b**
5.1e Skillmaster: comparison of adjectives — 1 **AT4/5a; ATs1-4**
5.1f Skillmaster: comparison of adjectives — 2 **AT4/5a; ATs1-4**
5.1g Skillmaster: letter writing **AT3/5a**
5.1h compound words **AT4/5a; AT2/5d**
5.1i fact find: people and places **AT2/5d**

Listening skills:
5.1j main idea/cause and effect — *The Runaway Summer* by Nina Bawden. **AT2/5b**
Side 1, track 1 Tape counter _____
5.1k looking for evidence **AT2/5b**
Sheet 5.1j links directly with the cassette. The answers may be found on the answer cards in the appendices.

The extract from *The Runaway Summer* is reproduced on activity sheet **5.1k** to allow for a closer examination of the text. It is not essential for the pupil to hear the track again, although it may be helpful if s/he were to do so.

5.1l listening for detail/recognition of same idea in different words **AT2/5b**
Side 1, track 2. Tape counter _____
There are two tasks on the activity sheet, and it is essential that each pupil listens to the tape at least twice.

The first time through s/he is asked to fill in on the street plan the names of Mrs. Tamworth's neighbours.

During the second playing, which may be interrupted using the pause button, the pupil should underline the sentences on the sheet which best match the description of the neighbours.

The exact words on the cassette are not given on the sheet, the task being to find sentences which say the same thing in a different way.

As preparation it may be advisable to make sure the group understand the meaning of these idiomatic expressions:
riding a high horse; silver tongued; butter wouldn't melt in his mouth; as different as chalk and cheese; getting into hot water; apple of my eye; salt of the earth; a peppery individual; great minds think alike; a chip off the old block.

The answers may be found on the answer cards in the appendices.

Group Prediction:

Activity sheets **5.1a-5.1d** feature *The Emerald Necklace,* one of four group prediction stories specially written for Level 5.

What is Group Prediction?

Group prediction is a teacher-led group activity developing both thinking and speaking skills. It encourages the children:

a) to examine a text carefully in order to make predictions about its eventual outcome;

b) to express their opinions and defend them when challenged;

c) to evaluate critically these predictions and inferences by re-examining the details of the text, both explicit and implicit;

d) to modify these predictions as and when appropriate.

Using the Stories

Experience has shown that the optimum group size is between eight and twelve.

Part One should be read carefully and the questions discussed. Opinions should be expressed, criticised and if necessary modified. Predictions should be made which fit the evidence of the text. There may be several possible outcomes at this stage. When reasoned predictions have been made, the next part of the story may be read. This could follow directly in the same session or saved for another lesson.

After a careful reading of the final part the children will be able to assess how close they were to the outcome of the story. It may well be that none of their predictions is close to its actual development. However, as long as their predictions have been carefully reasoned from the text, they may be equal, or indeed superior, to the writer's ending. Group prediction is therefore very useful in developing children's ideas about writing stories.

A re-examination of the earlier text is encouraged at the end of each story. This allows the children to spot missed clues, comment on any red herrings and examine mistaken inferences. This is even more useful if the teacher has made tape-recordings of the earlier sessions.

Speaking and listening: AT1/5b

1 *Friends* Talk about friends. Are the children's friends of any particular age/sex/race groups? Are the children conscious of this when they choose their friends? Use of the Level 4 activity sheet **4.1g** may help to focus the children's attention on their choice of friends.

Write a play about making friends. Place the emphasis on using natural language. The playlets may then be acted out and/or recorded as radio plays. **AT3/5a**

2 *Pen Friends* Pen friends give two vital ingredients for good writing: purpose and audience. Many teachers have found it extremely useful to link up with other schools (even abroad) for exchanges of letters. Alternatively write to pen friend agencies for their lists. **AT3/5a**

3 *Improvisation* Split the children into pairs or small groups. Improvise scenes such as these:—

a) two strangers introducing themselves

b) a gang of children with someone wanting to join them

c) a group of children electing a leader

d) a group of children expelling a member

Some important discussion points can be brought out of this improvised work i.e. What is friendship based on? What qualities do children look for in a leader? etc.

Emphasis does not have to be placed on gangs as being bad. 'Good' gangs and clubs should be explored too. **AT1/5b & d**

4 *Childsplay* Follow up the work on defining friendship with a game of *Childsplay.* Ask children to define certain abstract words, objects and personalities.

Present the definitions to a panel of 'competitors' to see if they can work out what is being defined. **AT1/5b**

5 *Bullying* Make use of the children's own experiences. Have they ever been bullied? Have they ever bullied anyone else? Why? How did they feel?

What sort of people do the children think make bullies? This should lead on to work on stereotypes. **AT1/5a & b**

6 *Dilemmas* Present the group with different situations and dilemmas to which they must react:

You find your best friend is stealing from children in your class. What do you do?

A friend confides in you that he/she is being bullied, but is afraid of repercussions if s/he tells anyone in authority. What would you do?

You suspect one of your close friends/relatives is taking drugs. What would you do? **AT1/5a, b & d**

7 *Relationships with Adults* How do the children get along with adults? Do adults always take notice of the children's opinions. Do the children ever feel excluded, ignored, insignificant? Why do they feel these difficulties exist? Can they be resolved in any way? **AT1/5a & b**

8 *Handicapped People* How do the children react when meeting handicapped people? Can they explain their feelings? Do they enjoy talking to handicapped people? Remember: handicapped people hate other people talking down to them.

How do the children think they would cope if they were handicapped in some way e.g. confined to a wheelchair? What would they like people to do for them? What would they prefer to do themselves?

How easy is it to get around in a wheelchair? What can be done to make it easier?

What other handicaps are there? Is it harder for other people to appreciate if the handicap is invisible e.g. deafness? **AT1/5a & b**

9 *Outward Appearances* Act out different facial expressions: surprised, worried, happy, frightened, etc. Can the children guess what feelings are being expressed? How is our judgement of other people affected by how they look, what they tell us, what other people say about them, tone of voice, attitude, mood etc.? **AT1/5b**

10 *Body Language* Follow up the work on facial expressions with a discussion of body language: how the voice may be saying one thing, but the body sending out different signals. What can we learn about a person from his body language?

Can the children convey feelings in body language while deliberately concealing them in their voices and facial expressions? **AT1/5b**

11 *Discussion* Encourage the discussion of controversial subjects:

Are men superior to women?
Are you racist/sexist?
AT1/5a, b, c & d

12 *Who Is It?* Each child chooses a famous person and uses the reference library to find out a number of facts about him/her. He then gives the facts one at a time to the rest of the group until they guess who it is. **AT1/5a & c; AT2/5d**

13 *Opinions* Reference is made in the book to the idea that the world would be uninteresting if we all thought the same. Do the children agree with this? Might this be the only way to achieve world peace?

Are opinions valid without real knowledge? What is an informed opinion? **AT1/5a & b**

14 *Opinion Polls* Discuss who uses opinion polls. How effective are they? Are they valuable/believable? Do they influence as well as reflect opinions? **AT1/5a & b**

Follow up work:

1 *Hodson's Yard* Ask the children to write an account of Bill Craddock's meeting with Jane as if they were witnesses to the scene in Hodson's yard.
AT3/5a, b & e

2 *Expressive Writing* The children's expressive writing of their own experiences of bullying and teasing can make very poignant reading. Their writing is often very honest and revealing. **AT3/5a & b**

3 *Ink Blot Patterns* Make a series of ink blot patterns and then ask the group what they can see in the various shapes.

This may be used as a starting point for appreciating how people see things differently. This technique is of course sometimes used in psychology for personality assessment work.

Creative work — poems and stories — may be written about the ink blots. The work may then be mounted to form an attractive display. **AT3/5a**

4 *Idioms*   Use the different responses from the work on ink blots to open discussion on idiomatic expressions such as 'one man's meat is another man's poison' and 'beauty is in the eye of the beholder'. Make lists of other idioms and their meanings.   **AT1/5a & b**

5 *Venn Diagrams*   Make Venn diagrams about pets, favourite pop stars, magazines, etc.   **AT3/5a**

Name_____

ENGLISH
ALIVE

Level 5
Master

5.1a

The Emerald Necklace: Part 1

The Fairbank Hotel at Sandy Bay hardly ever needed to advertise. Most of the time it was fully booked with satisfied guests, many of whom returned again and again. Mrs. Mason had worked hard for twenty years building up the hotel's high reputation.

One morning she was serving breakfast when Mrs. Channing, a regular guest, stopped her.

'Mrs. Mason, just look what Mr. Channing bought me yesterday.' She was wearing a most splendid emerald necklace. Privately, Mrs. Mason thought it was far too flashy for breakfast, but she said,

'Why, it's beautiful, Mrs. Channing! How kind of you Mr. Channing.'

'It's not as expensive as it looks,' said Mr. Channing.

'But still expensive,' pointed out his wife.

'It was in the sale at *Carruthers*, the jewellers on High Street. He had three of them. Absolute bargains, really. Closing down sale apparently.'

Mrs. Mason moved on to the next table. She was quite envious of Mrs. Channing. Secretly she felt the necklace would suit her much better. 'It would match my eyes,' she said to herself. The guest she was serving looked up at her.

'Did you say something?' he asked. Mrs. Mason flushed.

'I'm sorry, Mr. Rudge,' she smiled, 'I was talking to myself.' She moved on wondering what Mr. Rudge must think of her. He was a new guest, what she referred to as a "first timer".

'Mustn't put off first timers,' she thought.

That afternoon Mrs. Channing came bursting into her little office.

'Mrs. Mason, a dreadful thing has happened! My emerald necklace has gone!'

Mrs. Mason's heart sank.

'Have you mislaid it in the hotel?' she asked.

'It's not mislaid, Mrs. Mason, it's stolen!'

To think and write about

1   What have you learned about Mrs. Mason? How do you think she feels about the missing necklace? What do you think she will do about it? Give reasons for your answers.

2   What do you think of Mrs. Channing? What do you think Mrs. Mason feels about her? What makes you think so?

3   Do you think the necklace really has been stolen? What other possibilities can your group think of? Which one do you think the most likely?

5.1a   Group prediction — 1
© 1990 Collins Educational
AT1/5b; AT2/5b

The Emerald Necklace: Part 2

Mrs. Mason tried to calm Mrs. Channing. 'Perhaps your necklace had a faulty catch, and slipped off? Maybe outside the hotel?'

'No, Mr. Channing advised me not to wear it outside. I left it in a drawer in our room. I think we should call the police.'

'Why don't you have one last look first?' suggested Mrs. Mason.

As the Channings went off muttering, a terrible thought took shape in her mind. She began to think about Mr. Rudge. He had seen Mrs. Channing showing off her necklace. Her regular guests were above suspicion, but Mr. Rudge was a first timer, a stranger. All she knew about him was that he came from Peterborough and was booked in for two nights. He had gone out after breakfast, returned for lunch, and was now out again.

Mrs. Mason then did a thing she had never done before. She ran upstairs and began to search a guest's room. At the bottom of a drawer in Mr. Rudge's room she found the emerald necklace. She removed it and set off down the corridor to the Channing's room. As she turned a corner near the top of the stairs she almost bumped into a returning Mr. Rudge.

'Oh, I do beg your pardon, Mrs. Mason,' he said, but she was too shocked to speak. He went down the corridor and entered his room.

The Channings' room was empty. Mrs. Mason hurried down to her office.

'We've found it, Mrs. Mason,' an overjoyed Mrs. Channing greeted her. 'It was in my handbag all the time!'

Mrs. Mason collapsed into her chair.

To think and write about

1 Have you changed your opinion of Mrs. Mason? Do you think she was right to search Mr. Rudge's room? What would you have done?

2 What do you think will happen when Mr. Rudge finds his necklace is missing? What do you think Mrs. Mason will do then?

3 What would you like to see happen? Can you give a reason for your answer?

5.1b Group prediction — 2
© 1990 Collins Educational
AT1/5b; AT2/5b

Name _____

ENGLISH
ALIVE

Level 5
Master

5.1c

The Emerald Necklace: Part 3

The Channings left, bubbling with delight, but Mrs. Mason sat in despair, expecting that at any moment Mr. Rudge would come tearing downstairs to announce his necklace stolen.

How could she explain it?

'I took your necklace because I thought you had stolen it.' No that wouldn't do. 'I took it for safe-keeping. It was very foolish of you to leave such a valuable item in your room, you know. How did I know it was there? Why I went to look for it. I mean I just happened to open your drawer and find it hidden under a sweater.' No, that would be even worse.

She was so deep in thought that when Mr. Rudge spoke to her she nearly jumped out of her chair.

'I seem to have mislaid something, Mrs. Mason,' he was saying. 'You haven't seen my reading glasses, have you?' He had to repeat the question before she understood. In her mind's eye she could see them on the coffee table in the lounge where he had left them after lunch. She went to get them for him, but she walked as if in a dream.

Mr. Rudge thanked her for them and went back to his room.

'I could have told him,' she said to herself, 'I should have told him. I can never explain this properly now. My reputation is gone forever!'

To think and write about
Here are some thoughts Class 5 had about the story.

> "I think Mrs. Mason should own up and give back the necklace."
> "She can't. Whatever she says she'll seem dishonest."
> "She's not dishonest, she's just foolish."
> "She will be dishonest if she keeps it. She has to give it back."
> "I think she'll put it back when Mr. Rudge comes down for tea."
> "It seems to me Mr. Rudge is rather dopey. I would have checked it was still there as soon as I got back to the room."
> "I think that's just what he's going to do."

Which of these ideas do you agree with? Has your group any other ideas? Talk about them. What do you think will happen next?

5.1c Group prediction — 3
© 1990 Collins Educational
AT1/5b; AT2/5b

The Emerald Necklace: Part 4

The peace of the Fairbank hotel was shattered by the fire bell. Mrs. Mason stood at the bottom of the stairs assuring the guests that it was merely a fire drill. If they would kindly wait on the terrace she would check that everyone had left the building safely. They could return to their rooms as soon as she pronounced it safe to do so.

As the last guest left the hotel she rushed upstairs and returned the necklace to Mr. Rudge's drawer. Then smiling at her cleverness she went back downstairs and on to the terrace.

'The drill is over,' she said. 'You may all go back inside. Thank you for your co-operation.'

Mr. Rudge made for the stairs and then turned back.

'A word please, Mrs. Mason.' She took him into her office, afraid of what he might say. Perhaps he had looked for the necklace when the fire-bell rang. Of course, that must be it. That's what she would have done. How stupid of her not to think of it.

'I would like to compliment you on such a well-run hotel,' he began. 'You see I'm an hotel inspector for the *Best Small Hotels in Britain Guide* and the Fairbank will undoubtedly appear in the Highly Recommended section. You serve excellent food, and all your guests sing your praises, Mrs. Mason.'

He paused and looked a little more serious. 'By the way, I have a rather expensive necklace upstairs. I overheard the Channings discussing the sale at *Carruthers* and went along after breakfast to get a present for my wife. Do you think I could keep it in the hotel safe? I shall feel much happier knowing it is there.'

'So will I, Mr. Rudge,' Mrs. Mason replied with feeling, 'So will I!'

To think and write about

1   Is this how you thought the story would end? Did you expect Mrs. Mason to solve her problem so easily? What do you think of her now? How much of the happy ending was due to her quick thinking and how much to luck?

2   Did you enjoy the story? Would you have written it differently? Do you think the story would have been better if Mrs. Mason had been found out? Can you say why?

5.1d Group prediction — 4
© 1990 Collins Educational
AT1/5b; AT2/5b

Comparing Things — 1

The man is *tall*.   The elephant is *taller*.   The giraffe is the *tallest*.

The words in italics above are all **adjectives** (describing words).

Adjectives have three degrees of comparison: positive, comparative and superlative.

Tall is known as a *positive* adjective. Its job is to describe things.

Taller is a *comparative* adjective and is used when two things are being compared. It is formed by adding *-er* to the positive adjective: tall-*er*, fast-*er*.

Tallest is a *superlative* adjective and is used when describing more than two objects. It is formed by adding *-est* to the positive adjective: tall-*est*, fast-*est*.

---

1 Make comparative adjectives by adding *-er* to these adjectives.

cold _____   long _____   clean _____   sharp _____

thick _____   low _____   high _____   slow _____

2 Make superlative adjectives by adding *-est* to these adjectives.

dull _____   bright _____   wild _____   hard _____

soft _____   rough _____   smooth _____   loud _____

---

a) Very short adjectives often double the last consonant when adding *-er* or *-est*.
big bi**gg**er bi**gg**est   fat fa**tt**er fa**tt**est

b) If the adjective ends in *-y*, change the *y* to *-ier* or *-iest*.
pretty prett*ier* prett*iest*

---

3 Make these adjectives comparative.

tidy _____   jolly _____   hot _____   fit _____

noisy _____   heavy _____   busy _____   thin _____

4 Make these adjectives superlative.

friendly _____   big _____   happy _____   easy _____

sad _____   pretty _____   merry _____   cosy _____

5.1e Skillmaster — 1
© 1990 Collins Educational
AT4/5a; ATs1-4

Comparing Things — 2

The comparative of a long adjective is formed by adding *more* in front of it.

| *more* beautiful   *more* reliable   *more* exciting |

The superlative of a long adjective is formed by adding *most* in front of it.

| *most* beautiful   *most* reliable   *most* exciting |

1   Complete this list of adjectives.

Positive	Comparative	Superlative
thoughtful	more thoughtful	_____
graceful	_____	most graceful
alarming	_____	_____
_____	more amusing	_____
serious	_____	_____
amazing	_____	_____
comfortable	_____	_____
_____	_____	most expensive

2   Some adjectives have a different word for the comparative and superlative forms. You will have to learn these.

Positive	Comparative	Superlative
good	better	best
bad	worse	worst
little	less	least
some } many } much }	more	most

3   Choose three comparative adjectives and three superlatives from each list. Put each one in a sentence below.

_____

_____

_____

_____

_____

_____

5.1f Skillmaster — 2
© 1990 Collins Educational
AT4/5a; AT51-4

Name _____

Letter Writing

When you are writing a letter you should first ask yourself these questions:

> a) To whom am I writing the letter?
> b) Why will he/she be reading it?
> c) How shall I set it out?

Keep these in mind as you answer the following:

1 On which side of the paper do you write your address?

_____

2 What should you include in your letter after you have written your address and postcode?

_____

3 Where exactly should you begin writing your letter? _____

_____

4 If you don't know the name of the person to whom you are writing, how do you open your letter?

_____

5 If you were to begin your letter "Dear Sir," how would you sign off?

_____

6 How would you sign off if you knew the person to whom you were writing?

_____

7 You are inviting a friend to your birthday party. How would you begin?

Dear _____

_____

_____

8 You are writing to a T.V. company asking to take part in a quiz show. What would you write?
Dear Sir/Madam,

_____

_____

_____

_____

9 On a separate sheet of paper write out a full letter (including address) to *one* of the following:
   a) your best friend informing him/her of a holiday you are going on;
   b) your parents after you have arrived safely at your holiday resort;
   c) the holiday organiser, complaining about some aspect of your holiday;
   d) the holiday organiser, thanking him for an enjoyable holiday.

5.1g Skillmaster
© 1990 Collins Educational
AT3/5a

Name _____

ENGLISH
ALIVE

Level 5
Master

5.1h

New Words From Old

A New words can be made by joining two words together to make a compound word:

| beehive | keyhole | daydream |

1 Make as many words as you can by joining any two of these words together.

| step | finger | foot | print | nail | ladder |

_____ _____

2 Do the same with these.

| light | maid | shade | milk | house |
| keeper | man | green | sun | day |

_____ _____

_____ _____

3 Use the new words you have made to fill in
these blanks.

_____ _____

a) The milk was delivered by the _____ .

b) The lady painted her long, elegant _____ .

c) The tropical plants were grown in a _____ .

d) The burglar used a _____ to reach the high window, but he left a clear

set of _____ .

e) The butler sent the _____ to open the curtains so the

_____ could shine into the room.

B Some compound words are made from words joined together with a hyphen:

| brother-in-law | anti-clockwise | cold-blooded |

Such compound words are listed in a dictionary
in alphabetical order of the first word in the compound:

| anti-clockwise, brother-in-law, cold-blooded. |

1 List these compound words in alphabetical order. Use the back of this sheet for answers.

double-cross	bird's-eye-view	tug-of-war
daughter-in-law	trap-door	world-wide
brief-case	vice-captain	sky-blue

2 Put each one of these compound words into a sentence of your own.

| old-fashioned | fire-escape | car-park | passer-by |
| well-meaning | letter-box | round-the-clock | mouse-trap |

5.1h Compound words
© 1990 Collins Educational
AT4/5a; AT2/5d

Name _____

ENGLISH
ALIVE

Level 5
Master

5.1i

People and Places

Use an encyclopedia and other reference books to find the names of these famous people and places.
Useful hint: underline the **key words** in each question and use these to help you in your search.

1 The founder of Islam was born in this holy city.

   Person _____ Place _____

2 The king who ordered the writing of the Domesday Book won an important battle here.

   Person _____ Place _____

3 Where a famous Italian got the idea for the pendulum, and where a leaning tower can be seen.

   Person _____ Place _____

4 This island was awarded the George Cross in 1942. Who were its famous knights?

   People _____ Place _____

5 The father of printing in Britain set up his press here.

   Person _____ Place _____

6 A Scotsman found a great waterfall on this river and named it Victoria Falls.

   Person _____ River _____

7 This famous explorer entered Kublai Khan's city in 1275.

   Person _____ Place _____

5.1i Fact find
© 1990 Collins Educational
AT2/5d

Name _____

ENGLISH
ALIVE

Level 5
Master

5.1j

Listening for the Main Idea

1 Which of these is the main idea of the extract from *The Runaway Summer?*
Underline the correct answer.
   a) Mary is angry.   **b)** Mary hates vests.   **c)** Mary is rude to Aunt Alice.

2 Invent a good title for the passage. *Remember: it should tell what the main idea is.*

_____

Cause and Effect
Answer in sentences.

1 What was it about Aunt Alice that most annoyed Mary? _____

_____

2 What caused Mary to be so angry on this particular occasion? _____

_____

3 Why had Mary eaten her porridge? _____

_____

4 Why do you think Mary was eager to please her grandfather? _____

_____

5 Why exactly does Mary hate her vest so much? _____

_____

6 What caused her grandfather to play with his right ear? _____

_____

7 What effect did this have on Mary? _____

_____

5.1j Listening skills
© 1990 Collins Educational
AT2/5b

From *The Runaway Summer* by Nina Bawden

Mary was angry. She had been angry for ages: she couldn't remember when she had last felt nice. Sometimes she was angry for a good reason — when someone tried to make her do something she didn't want to do — but most of the time she was angry for no reason at all. She just woke in the morning feeling cross and miserable and as if she wanted to kick or break things.

Aunt Alice could make her angry just by being there, with her rabbity face and grey hair in a bun and the little tuft of spiky beard on her chin that waggled when she talked; and her teeth that made a clicking sound at mealtimes, and her stomach that sometimes made a noise in between — a watery suck and gurgle like the last of the bath running out. And when *she* tried to make Mary do something she didn't want to do, it made Mary so cross that she grew hot inside.

This morning, Aunt Alice wanted Mary to wear her woollen vest. It was such a lovely July day, with the wind blowing and the small clouds scudding, that Mary had been in a better mood than usual when she came down to breakfast. She had even eaten her porridge because she knew her grandfather believed it was good for her. When he saw her empty plate, he had beamed over his newspaper and said, 'Well, it looks as if our good sea air is giving you an appetite at last,' and seemed so pleased, as if in eating a plateful of porridge Mary had done something quite remarkably good and clever, that she wondered what else she could do. She thought she might say, 'I think I'll go down to the sea and skim stones after breakfast,' because she knew this would please her grandfather too: he worried when she did what he called 'moping indoors'.

And now Aunt Alice had spoiled everything by asking Mary if she had put on her woollen vest!

'That jersey's not thick enough for this treacherous weather,' she said, looking nervously at the window as if the weather were a dangerous dog that might suddenly jump through it and bite her.

Mary scowled and felt her face go solid and lumpy like a badly made pudding.

'It's not cold,' she said. 'And I'm hot *now*. If I put my vest on, I'll be boiling to *death*.'

'There's quite a wind out. It's blowing up cold. I know I'm wearing *my* vest! Just between you and me and the gatepost!'

Mary looked carefully round the room. 'I don't see any gatepost,' she said.

Aunt Alice laughed in her high, silly way — not as if she were amused, but as if she were trying to apologise for something.

'It's just an expression, dear. Haven't you heard it before?'

'I've *heard* it all right, but I think it sounds potty,' Mary said, 'And I just *hate* those horrible old vests. They've got sleeves! Sleeves and *buttons!* I expect you knew I'd hate them, that's why you bought them for me!'

She stabbed her spoon into her boiled egg, and some of the yolk spattered out.

'Oh Mary,' Aunt Alice said in a sad, fading voice. Pale eyes bulging, nose twitching, she looked like a frightened rabbit.

Mary knew her aunt was frightened of her, and this made her more bad tempered than ever. It was so ridiculous for an old woman to be frightened of an eleven year old girl.

She said bitterly, 'No one else in the *whole world* wears vests with sleeves and buttons.'

Aunt Alice said, 'Oh Mary,' again. She sounded as if she were trying not to cry. Grandfather put down his newspaper and looked at her. Then he smiled at Mary.

'My dear child, someone must wear them or the shops wouldn't stock them, would they? It's a case of supply and demand. No demand, no supply.'

For a second, Mary almost smiled back at him. It was, indeed, quite difficult *not* to smile at her grandfather, who looked, with his round, rosy face, and round, blue eyes, rather like a cheerful, if elderly, baby. He was bald as a baby, too — balder than most, in fact: the top of his head was smooth and shiny as if Aunt Alice polished it every day when she polished the dining-room table. Usually, just to look at her grandfather made Mary feel nicer — a bit less cross, certainly — but now, after that first second, she felt worse, not better, because she saw that his blue eyes were puzzled and that he was playing with his right ear, folding the top over with his finger and stroking the back with his thumb. This was something he only did when he was thinking hard or worried about something, and Mary knew he was upset because she had been rude to Aunt Alice. Although this made her ashamed and miserable underneath, it made her angry on top.

1   Why do you think Mary is staying with her grandfather?

_____

_____

_____

2   Where do you think Mary's grandfather lives? What evidence can you find to support this?

_____

_____

3   What do you think Mary will do now? Continue the story on the back of this sheet.

Lavender Close

Mrs Tamworth

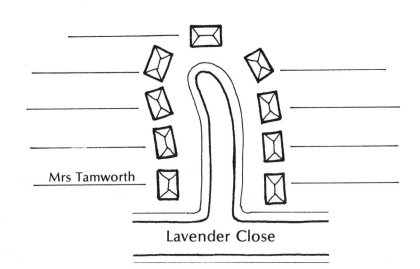

Mrs Tamworth

Lavender Close

A   Listen to side 1, track 2 of the listening skills cassette. Mrs. Tamworth will tell you where each of her neighbours lives. Write each name on the plan as she does so.

B   Listen to the cassette again. As Mrs. Tamworth describes each neighbour look for a similar description under the neighbour's picture.
   You will not find her exact words, but look for a description which says the same thing in different words.
Underline the matching description.

Mrs. Clark

She is rich.
She likes horses.
She is snooty.

Adam Meadows

He is well-behaved.
He looks angelic.
He is naughty.

Katie Hollins

She's always in trouble.
She is reliable.
She is hard-working.

Joanna Maxwell

She is very like Adam.
She is totally different from Adam.
She is a friend of Adam.

Rebecca Hollins

She is her father's favourite.
She gets on well with her father.
She annoys her father.

Gordon Davies

He likes money.
He's got a posh accent.
He can talk his way round people.

Dr. Bharti

He's younger than he looks.
He's just like his father.
He is his father's favourite.

Jacob Hollins

He's very dull.
He's well respected.
He's very quiet.

Mr. Gardener

He doesn't like Mrs. Tamworth.
He shares the same ideas
as Mrs. Tamworth.
He helps Mrs. Tamworth.

Mr. Hickard

He's very quick-tempered
He's old and frail.
He's charming and polite.

5.11   Listening skills
© 1990 Collins Educational
AT2/5b

Unit 2

Theme — Journeys
Stimuli — *Scott of the Antarctic* — account, diary extracts, photographs and map
from *The Diddakoi* — Rumer Godden, Macmillan
limericks
photographs as stimuli for verse
holiday brochures
from *The Machine Gunners*, Robert Westall, Macmillan (listening skills cassette)

AT1 Speaking/listening
5b-d problem solving
5d group presentation

ATs1-4 Word study
5* words from other languages
5* origins of place names
5* national names

AT2 Reading
Scott of the Antarctic:
5b — inference
5b — reading for detail
5b — imaginative response
5b — speculation
5d — re-telling contents of passage
5d — time line (sequencing)

Map of Antarctica:
5b — context clues
5b — speculation
5d — adding route
5d — use of reference books

Passage/Map of Amberhurst Village:
5b — reading passage for detail
5d — adding detail of map

Story of Our Language:
5b — context clues
5b & d — inference from maps
5d — use of reference books
5d — use of maps for reference
5b — speculation
5b — reasoning

Around the World:
5d — use of atlas

Time Quest:
5b — problem solving

Holidays — What's the Truth?:
5c — evaluation
5c — persuasion
5c-d — modelling: pictures
5d — use of brochures as reference material
5d — evaluation of same

Choosing a Holiday:
5b — reading for detail
5b-c — evaluation
5c-d — modelling: tree diagram
5d — finding facts from chart
5d — calculation from chart

Travelling:
5d use of reference material

AT3 Writing skills
Poetic:
5a postcard
5a-c, e description of holiday hotel
5a, d, e rhyming schemes
5a, d, e limericks
5a, d, e simile and metaphor poems from photographic stimuli
5a-e description of holiday from own experience

Transactional:
5a making a tree diagram
5a filling in holiday booking form
5a making own passport
5a graph
5a-c recording contents of a passage
5a-c, e recording solutions to problems
5a-c, e letter of complaint
5a-e giving directions/route
5a-e description of a journey: making booklet
5a-e drawing labelled diagrams
5a-e narrative, writer as participant
5a-e writing a holiday brochure
5a-e local guidebook
5a-e planning a world tour

Solutions to 'Time Quest' (pp. 26-7)
Problem 1: Who is Your Guide?
Since everyone received a different sentence then Hori will not be imprisoned, Mosi will not become your guide but Amon will become your bearer.

Since Mosi can now be neither your bearer nor your guide, he is the one who will be imprisoned and Hori becomes your guide.

Problem 2: Crossing the Nile
First you cross with the boatman.

Then leaving him on the far bank you bring the boat back.

You then take across Amon, the bearer, and leave him on the other side with the boatman.

You then return in the boat, collect the pack and recross the river.

You stay with the pack and the bearer, sending the boatman back for Hori.

You are now all safely across.

Problem 3: Who is Telling the Truth?
If the first villager were a truthful moon worshipper he would not deny it: therefore he does not worship the Moon God.

Since he is not a moon worshipper, he is telling the truth, and so cannot be a lying sun worshipper: he must therefore be a sky worshipper.

The second villager must then be a sun or moon worshipper. Either of these would deny being a sun worshipper, so we must look at the words of the third villager.

He says he is not a sky worshipper, which we know to be true. Since he is speaking the truth he must be a moon worshipper, and the second tribesman a sun worshipper.

The first villager therefore worships the Sky God, the second the Sun God and the third the Moon God. Since moon worshippers always tell the truth the correct path is the right-hand one.

Problem 4: Dividing the Diamonds
Another diamond needs to be borrowed. The Pharoah is then given half of them (9 diamonds), the second son a third (6 diamonds), and the third son his ninth (2 diamonds). The old Pharoah's seventeen diamonds have now been shared out according to his decree. The remaining, borrowed, diamond can now be returned to its kind lender.

Problem 5: Sending the Message
The answer to the Dividing the Diamonds problem must be written on a sheet of paper in invisible ink. The best ink will need to be found by experimentation. A method for reading it must also be worked out. The sheet must then be folded to make a paper aeroplane capable of travelling the correct distance, along a predictable path and flying at the necessary height.

Activity sheets:
5.2a   letter writing/railway timetable **AT2/5d; AT3/5a**
5.2   giving directions: street plan **AT2/5d; AT3/5a**
5.2c   Amberhurst Village: adding details to map (Links with page 21 of pupil's book.) **AT2/5d**
5.2d   *Treasure Hunt:* context clues/use of maps **AT2/5d**
5.2e   people and their countries: use of reference library **AT2/5d**

5.2f   holiday booking form (Links with page 31 of pupil's book.) **AT2/5d; AT3/5a**
5.2g   *World Traveller:* using reference material **AT2/5d**
5.2h   sorting **AT2/5d**
5.2i   *The Story of Our Language:* word study (Links with pages 22-3 of pupil's book.) **AT2/5d**
5.2j   prefixes: *en-, for-, con-, sub-* **AT4/5a**
5.2k   Skillmaster: simple past tense helping verb **ATs1-4**

Listening skills:
5.2l   aural memory: recall of detail: *The Machine Gunners* **AT2/5b**
Side 2, track 3.   Tape counter _____
This extract from *The Machine Gunners* by Robert Westall tells of Chas' discovery of the tail section of a Heinkel He 111 bomber. There are questions on the activity sheet to test recall of detail and an opportunity to predict what might happen next.

The answers appear on the answer card in the appendices.

5.2m   points of view/fact and opinion **AT2/5b-c**
Side 1, track 4. Tape counter _____
Two different points of view on the holiday resort of Shoreham are featured. The pupil is asked to list likes and dislikes, and to speculate on why the viewpoints should be so different.

The answers appear on the answer card in the appendices.

Speaking and listening:
1   *Drama: Adventure Road* **AT1/5a-d**
The aim here is to provide stimuli for the development of a series of adventures met with on a journey.

Large pieces of plain white paper, one for each child, should be laid on the floor to form a path with forks and branches. The group should then discuss their journey along this road. They should decide on an event for each sheet of paper e.g. meeting a giant, crossing a broken bridge, fighting a dragon, crossing a desert, etc. A picture to represent one of the events should then be drawn on each sheet of paper.

When the adventure road is complete the children should split into small groups and choose a route to follow. At each of the various stages they should improvise appropriate scenes and show how they solve the problems they are faced with.

in each pair a picture postcard, and his partner a similar-sized blank piece of paper. Each pair should then sit back to back. The person with the picture postcard should describe his card so that his partner may draw as accurate a copy as possible. When the drawing is complete the two pictures should be compared.

3 *Desert Trek* **AT1/5a, b, c & d**
An expedition is to make a trek across the Sahara. Suitable people need to be found, especially a competent leader. Both sexes should be represented.

Discuss the qualities, skills and experiences a leader should have, making reference to Scott and Amundsen (see pupil's book). Ask the children to prepare in groups a newspaper advertisement for members of the expedition.

Discuss the different priorities the children specify in the job description. Let them work out the questions they would ask at the interviews, and also what they would answer. Act out the interviews in role play.

4 *Points of View* **AT1/5a**
Ask the children to recall what they can of school trips, outings or holidays they have been on. Do they all remember the same things? Do they use the same language to describe different elements of the outing? Did they enjoy it equally? Can they say why? Compare their viewpoints with the ones expressed on the listening skills cassette, side 1 track 4. Are any of their views as different as those expressed on the cassette?

Follow-up activities:

1 *Letter Writing* **AT3/5a**
A project on other countries may encourage good letter-writing skills. Ask the children to write to embassies or national tourist boards for information on their countries. The children will find it rewarding to see the wide variety of information which their letters will bring.

2 *Phrase Books* **AT2/5d; AT3/5a & e**
Let the children use simple texts and holiday brochures to make a simple phrase book for a country of their choice. Words to include are: please, thank you, doctor, water, telephone, how much, no, yes, one, two, etc.

3 *Travel Posters* **AT2/5d**
Design travel posters which not only show a country in its best light, but also some of the personality of its people.

4 *Flags and National Costume* **AT2/5d**
Make a display of the flags and national costume of other countries. Design a national costume for Great Britain (male and female).

5 *Food Around the World* **AT2/5d**
No look at other countries would be complete without trying some of the foods they have to offer. Plan a route around the world and then select some typical foodstuffs from each country on the tour. Find recipes from these countries and prepare one or more dishes.

6 *Long Distance Travel* **AT2/5d**
Imagine what it was like making a journey round the world many years ago. Today we can travel to Australia in hours; one hundred years ago it took months. Find out about settlers/convicts being transported to America and Australia. What were travelling conditions like? Compare them with today.

7 *Famous Journeys* **AT1/5a-d**
Discuss famous journeys from history: voyages of discovery, journeys into space, etc.

8 *Fictional Journeys* **AT2/5a & b**
Read about fictional journeys: *The Wizard of Oz* (along the Yellow Brick Road), *The Incredible Journey, I Am David, The Hobbit, Journey to the Centre of the Earth*, etc.

9 *Charity Walks* **AT2/5d**
In Britain, many people make journeys to raise money for charity, e.g. walking from John O'Groats to Land's End. Ask the children to locate these two places on the map, and calculate the distance between them. **Maths AT8/5a**

10 *Wreckers' Rock* is the fifth in the *Adventures in English* series and provides follow up work for this unit.

It consists of a book of 28 Pressure-fax activity sheets and a computer program in which the children use detective work to discover and thwart the plans of a gang of modern-day wreckers. It gives experience in decision making, problem solving and research skills.

Full details of *Wreckers' Rock* and the *Adventures in English* series can be found in the appendices.

Name _____

ENGLISH
ALIVE

Level 5
Master

5.2a

10 Seaview Crescent,
Highcliffe,
Linnshire,
HCI 6ZZ
Monday, 10th August

Dear Bobby,

I hope you are enjoying your holiday as much
as I am. I can't wait to see you at the
weekend and hear all about it.

I enclose the timetable from Whitbridge to
Highcliffe. Try to come on Saturday, but if
you can't, do make sure you're here by
2 pm on Sunday, because that's when
my party is. Please let us know which
train you're coming on so we can
meet you at the station.

Love to your Mum and Dad.

Best wishes, Chris

Using the railway timetable write a reply to Chris's invitation saying precisely when you expect to arrive at Highcliffe Station.

	WO		WO	xSu		FO	xSu	Sum
Whitbridge	09.12	09.54	10.23	11.02	11.47	12.01	13.01	14.20
Kilmerton	09.22	10.04	. .	. .	11.57	. .	. .	. .
Great Hartley	09.29	10.11	. .	. .	12.04	12.16	. .	. .
Newby Ash	09.37	. .	. .	. .	12.12	. .	. .	. .
Vanbury Hill	09.44	10.24	10.47	11.22	12.19	12.29	13.17	14.42
Linnington......................	. .	10.28	. .	. .	12.24	. .	. .	. .
Highcliffe	09.56	10.43	11.02	. .	12.39	12.43	13.30	14.59
Seaport	. .	10.52	11.11	11.43	. .	12.52	13.39	. .

WO *Week days only*
FO *Fridays only*

xSu *Not Sunday*
Sum *May to September only*

Look at the timetable again and answer these questions.

1 Which is the last train you could catch at Whitbridge to arrive at
Highcliffe before 12.00 on a Saturday? _____

2 Which is the last train you could catch from Great Hartley
to arrive at Seaport before 15.00 on a Friday? _____

3 Which train travels from Whitbridge to Seaport in the shortest time? _____

4 Which train would you catch to travel from Kilmerton to Newby Ash on a Sunday? _____

5 How long would you have to wait at Vanbury Hill if you have missed the 11.22 train? _____

6 Which is the last train which would get you from Whitbridge to Vanbury Hill by 15.00 in December?

_____

Name _____

ENGLISH
ALIVE

Level 5
Master

5.2b

Planning a Route

This street plan of Highcliffe shows the railway station and Chris's house. Describe the most direct route by car between the two if there were no road works blocking Hartley Street.

Now describe a new route allowing for the road works detour.

Highcliffe

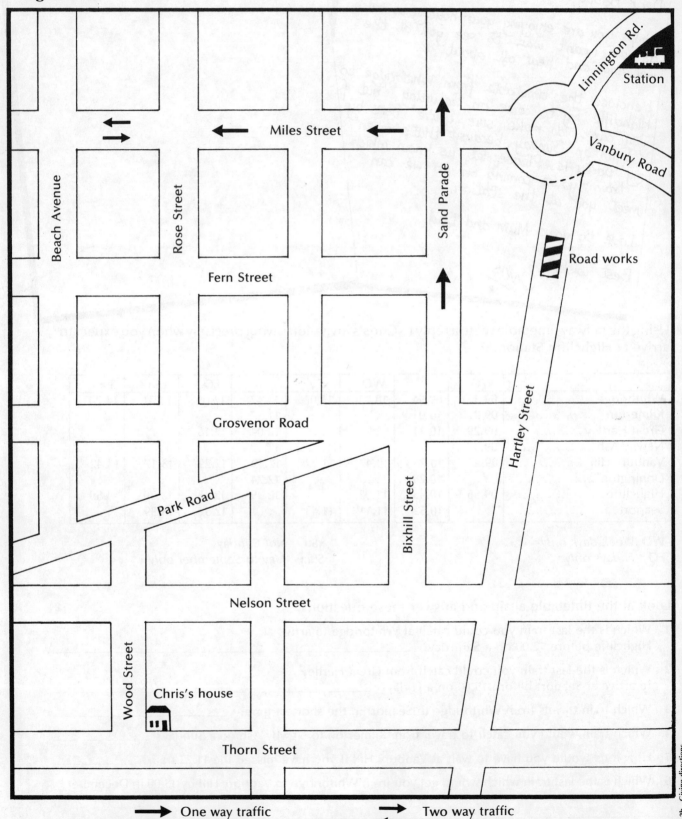

→ One way traffic   ⇄ Two way traffic

Name _____

Amberhurst Village

Read the description of Amberhurst village on page 21 of *English Alive* Book 5. Then label the places on the map.

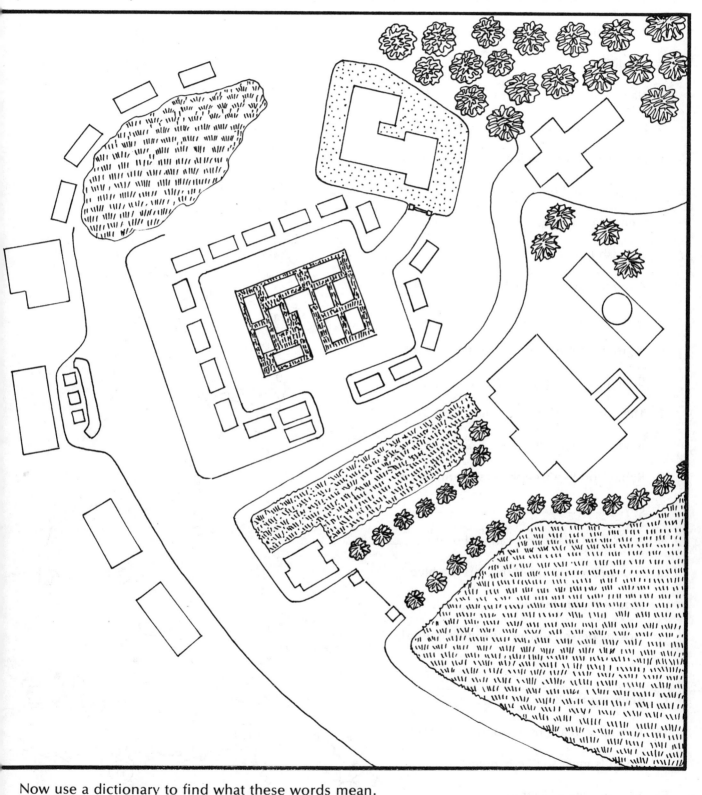

Now use a dictionary to find what these words mean.

cupola _____   knoll _____

common _____   avenue _____

lodge _____

To find the treasure you will need to identify the fourteen locations numbered on the map. Think about the clues, and then use atlases and road maps to help you. Good luck.

1 River which runs through Roman Londinium. _____

2 Name the waterway over which stands the largest single-span suspension bridge. _____

3 It is famed for its capital rock and a tattoo you'll not find on anyone's arm. _____

4 Sounds more like an item of knitwear than a Welsh town. _____

5 An alternative to football was invented at a school here. _____

6 A group of islands off the north coast of Britain. _____

7 The home of the world's most famous tennis tournament. _____

8 Robin Hood's adversary was Sheriff of this city. _____

9 A Channel island you can pull over. _____

10 A district of Liverpool that has the blue scouse football team. _____

11 Not the person's island, the other one. Isle of _____

12 Town on the River Exe. _____

13 Can there really be a reptile at mainland Britain's most southerly point? _____

14 Shakespeare's birthplace. _____

_____

Take the first letter of each of your answers in order, and they will spell out the treasure you have found!

5.2d Treasure Hunt
© 1990 Collins Educational
AT2/5d

Name _____

ENGLISH
ALIVE

Level 5
Master

5.2e

People and their Countries Use Atlases and Reference books to help you complete this chart.

Country	People	Official Language	Capital City	Currency	Head of State
Britain	British	English	London	£ Sterling	
France					
Egypt					
Australia					
USA					
Canada					
India					
USSR					
Japan					
China					
Spain					
South Africa					
Saudia Arabia					
Pakistan					
New Zealand					
Italy					
Greece					
Afghanistan					
Netherlands					

Name _____

ENGLISH
ALIVE

Level 5
Master

5.2f

Holiday Booking Form

Flight Details

Departure Airport: _____ Holiday Code: _____
Destination Airport: _____
Departure Date: _____ Day: _____ No. of Nights: _____
Country/Island: _____ Resort: _____
Hotel/Apartment: _____ Full Board ☐ Half Board ☐
                                    Bed & Breakfast ☐ Room Only ☐

Passenger Details

Total no. in party: _____   Children: _____

Mr/Mrs/Ms	Initials	Surname	Age if under 18	Insurance
				Yes
				Yes
				Yes
				Yes
				Yes
				Yes

Address: Emergency contact:

Tel: Tel:

Special Holiday Offers

Singles Holiday	
3 Weeks for price of 2	
Gulet Holiday	
Two Centre Holiday	

Other Requests: (Please state)

Other Requirements

Skycot	
Mountain View	
Inland View	
Sea View	
Balcony	
View of pool	

Client's Name and Address for correspondence

PARADISE TRAVEL
ATBA 13729
22 SEAVIEW ROAD
SOUTHPORT
03 941 1234

Signature _____ Date _____

Travel Agent's Stamp

5.2f Holiday Booking Form
© 1990 Collins Educational
AT2/5d; AT3/5a

Name _____

World Traveller

You will need an atlas, an encyclopedia and other reference books to play this game.

As you answer each question write its number in the correct place on the map. For example when you have drawn a picture of an Easter Island stone figure in square 1, write 1 on the map to show where Easter Island is.

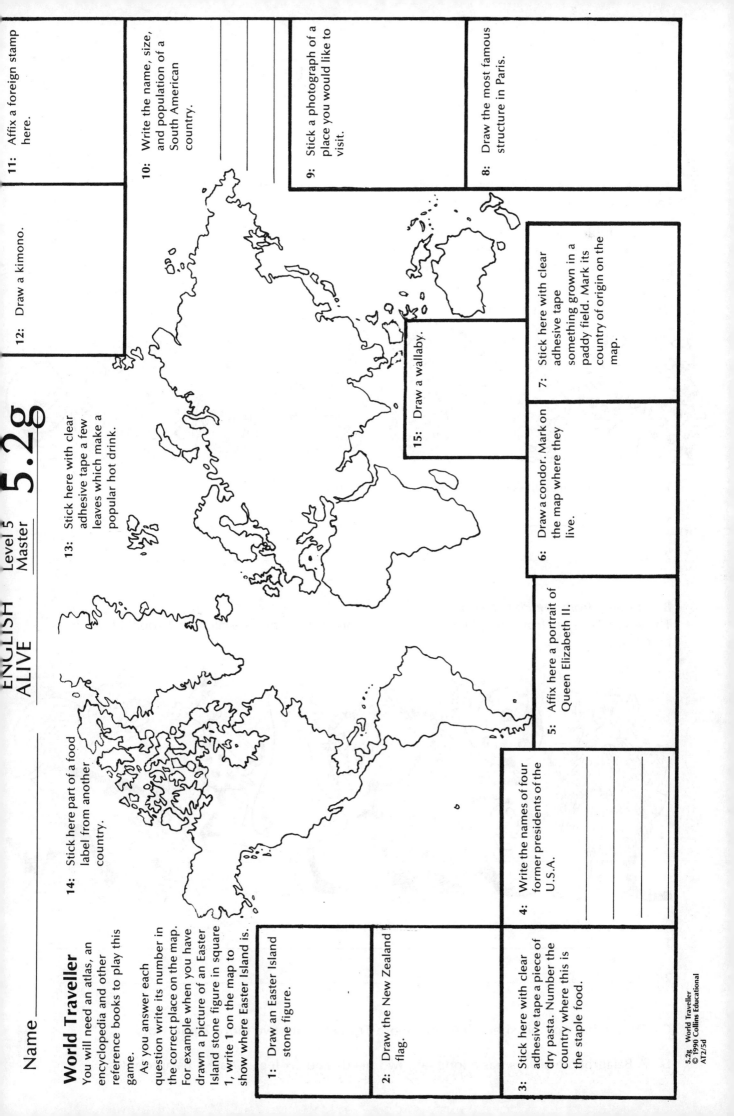

11: Affix a foreign stamp here.

12: Draw a kimono.

10: Write the name, size, and population of a South American country.

9: Stick a photograph of a place you would like to visit.

8: Draw the most famous structure in Paris.

13: Stick here with clear adhesive tape a few leaves which make a popular hot drink.

7: Stick here with clear adhesive tape something grown in a paddy field. Mark its country of origin on the map.

15: Draw a wallaby.

6: Draw a condor. Mark on the map where they live.

5: Affix here a portrait of Queen Elizabeth II.

14: Stick here part of a food label from another country.

4: Write the names of four former presidents of the U.S.A.

_____
_____
_____
_____

1: Draw an Easter Island stone figure.

2: Draw the New Zealand flag.

3: Stick here with clear adhesive tape a piece of dry pasta. Number the country where this is the staple food.

5.2g World Traveller
© 1990 Collins Educational
AT2/5d

Name _____

Aliens

A The two races on the planet Trongle are the Drumbles and the Zipperwots. They look very similar, but to tell them apart you need to remember this:

> A Drumble always has eyes on stalks, sometimes carries a handgun and has at least two antennae coming out of his head.

This is a Drumble:

Draw a ring round each Drumble in this picture.

Which two features make a Zipperwot different from a Drumble?

1 _____

2 _____

B *Trippets from the Planet Zong*
These are Trippets from the planet Zong. Write down two things which all Trippets have in common.

1 _____

2 _____

C On the back of this sheet draw five more Trippets, and five more Zipperwots.

D A Balagrobble always has a long tail, two heads and six legs. Draw 5 Balagrobbles.

5.2h Sorting
© 1990 Collins Educational
AT2/5d

Name_____

The Story of Our Language

You will need to read the section *The Story of Our Language* (Book 5, unit 2) before you attempt this sheet.

A   Sort these words according to their origin.

abbot	day	monk
altar	earth	night
awkward	husband	nobility
bailiff	hymn	parlour
beef	is	priest
chancellor	light	scale
curfew	man	you

Saxon	Latin	Viking	Norman French
_____	_____	_____	_____
_____	_____	_____	_____
_____	_____	_____	_____
_____	_____	_____	_____
_____	_____	_____	_____
_____	_____	_____	_____
_____	_____	_____	_____

B   Write a sentence for each of the following, explaining the part each played in the development of the English language.

1   The Angles, Saxons and Jutes _____

_____

2   St. Augustine _____

_____

3   King Alfred _____

_____

4   William Shakespeare _____

_____

...good dictionary to find out what these prefixes mean.

con-	en-	for-	sub-

Now put these words in the chart with their correct prefix. The first one has been done for you.

test	aqua	divide	go	fold	marine	ever
joy	sake	slave	front	give	circle	strain
way	bid	form	danger	junction	conscious	

con-	en-	for-	sub-
contest	en_____	for _____	sub_____
con_____	en_____	for _____	sub_____
con_____	en_____	for _____	sub_____
con_____	en_____	for _____	sub_____
con_____	en_____	for _____	sub_____

Choose *two* words from each of the columns of the chart and write them in sentences.

1 _____

2 _____

3 _____

4 _____

5 _____

6 _____

7 _____

8 _____

Now use a dictionary to help you find the correct meaning of these words. Underline the correct answer.

1 enable   to make able/to move/to disable
2 congenial   pleasant/runs in the family/not generous
3 subscribe   to re-write/to sign at the bottom/learn to write
4 forbear   to hold up/to make rules/to control oneself
5 submerge   to go underwater/to join together/to overlap
6 enrage   get older/infuriate/to quieten someone
7 forage   food and provisions/search out/to come of age
8 consignment   delivery/a prize given to a runner up/not changing
9 subcontinent   to contain/a division of class/a landmass smaller than a continent
10 entangle   to get ensnared/to sort out a tangle/to knot a rope

Past Tense

Complete this table.

Verb	Simple Past Tense	Past Tense with Helping Verb
* to fall * to do	he fell she _____	he has fallen she has _____
* to rise	it _____	it has _____
to _____	*we ate _____	*we have _____
* to give	I gave	I have _____
to take	they _____	they have _____
* to _____	it _____	it has sunk
* to see	they _____	they have _____
to ring	it _____	it has _____
to _____	she went	she _____ _____
to write	I _____	I _____ _____
to _____	it _____	it has bitten

Now complete these sentences using the correct form of the verb in brackets.

1 I _____ to town. My friends had _____ before me. (to go)

2 We _____ our last meal. We have _____ all our supplies.
   (to eat)

3 The dog _____ Jane's arm. It had _____ her on the leg too.
   (to bite)

4 I have _____ a letter in reply to the one my pen friend

   _____ to me. (to write)

5 He _____ your coat by mistake. He has _____ it home.
   (to take)

6 The burglar _____ a second candlestick to go with the one he had

   _____ the previous week. (to steal)

On the back of this sheet make up your own sentences to show the correct usage of the verbs
marked *.

5.2k Skillmaster
© 1990 Collins Educational
ATs1-4

The Machine Gunners

Answer these questions in as much detail as you can.

1 What was the boy's full name? _____

2 Where did he live? _____

3 What was the name of his school? _____

4 What kind of plane did the boy find? _____

_____

5 Into what kind of building had the aeroplane crashed? _____

_____

6 Describe the swastika painted on the plane. _____

_____

7 What was the gunner wearing on his head? _____

8 Which one of his eyes was missing? _____

9 Underline what was written on the little door in the plane.

   Nicht Verstehen   *Nicht Anfassen*   *Nicht Essen*

10 In which period is the story set? _____

    What makes you think so? _____

_____

11 At what time of year did these events take place? _____

    What makes you think so? _____

12 What do you think the boy will do now? Use the back of this sheet to write your ending to the story.

5.21 Listening skills
© 1990 Collins Educational
AT2/5b

Name _____

A Holiday in Shoreham

1 What did Jason like and dislike about Shoreham?

_____   _____

_____   _____

_____   _____

_____   _____

_____   _____

2 What did Molly like and dislike about Shoreham?

_____   _____

_____   _____

_____   _____

_____   _____

_____   _____

3 Why do you think their opinions are so different?

_____   _____

_____   _____

_____   _____

_____   _____

Look at these sentences. Were they spoken by Molly or Jason?
Match the sentence to its speaker.

Molly

Jason

'Its full of noisy amusement arcades.'	'It's got smashing beaches.'	'The beach has no pebbles.'
'The Sandcentre is a rip-off.'	'The zoo is the best in the country.'	'Three ugly piers.'
'Shoreham is a fantastic place.'	'The Pleasure Palace is expensive.'	'The log flume is the longest in the world.'
'The lights are gaudy and tacky.'	'The tide goes out a long way.'	
'The sea is dirty and polluted.'	'The trams are old fashioned sorts of bus.'	

Now underline the sentences that you think are facts.
Remember: A fact is something that is true.

5.2m Listening skills
© 1990 Collins Educational
AT2/5b-c

Unit 3

Theme — The Media
Stimuli — newspaper cuttings
              'News' by Aidan Chambers, from
              Funny Folk, Heinemann
              (listening skills cassette)
              'The Blind Men and the Elephant'
              by John Godfrey
              From *The TV Kid* — Betsy Byars,
              Bodley Head
              Article from *Early times* 27/4/88,
              written by Juliet Buckley, aged
              12

AT1 Speaking/listening
5a-c comparison of TV news with newspapers
5a-c evaluating TV viewing habits
5b evaluating news: what it is, different kinds of news, where it comes from, the different ways in which it is communicated to its audience
5b "News" (see listening cassette below):
— appreciation
— reasoning
— main idea
5b "The Blind Men and the Elephant" (see listening cassette below):
— points of view
— fact and opinion
— inference
— evaluation
— reasoning
5b-c conducting a survey
5b, d newspaper surveys
5b, d own chocolate bar:
— group presentation
— market research
— evaluation of results
— recording jingles
— recording TV advert
5c examining the media: information, entertainment and persuasion
5d planning a school newspaper
5d own TV advertisement

AT2 Reading
5a-b selecting news stories for specific audience
5a-d news on TV
5a, c letter of opinion
5b cloze passage
5b-c "TV Kid":
— speculation
— context clues
— inference
— imaginative response

5b-c, e TV advertisements:
— evaluation (using **5.3p**)
— recording as a story board (using **5.3q**)
5b-c, e poems on listening skills cassette
5b-c, e newspaper advertisements
5b, d classifying news stories
5b-d awareness that newspaper reports may be unintentionally misleading
5b-d examining facts
5c-d viewpoint
5c-d TV programme guide:
— reading for detail
— matching programmes to audience
— classification
— fact and opinion
5c-e detecting bias, selection of facts and distortion
5d search reading
5d topic sentences/the main idea
5d evaluating the relative importance of news stories
5d making up questions about news reports
5d reading a diagram

AT3 Writing
The writing process:
5b direct and reported speech
5d editing and improving writing
Poetic:
5a-e descriptive prose
5a-e expressing thoughts about TV programmes
5a-e — TV program review
Transactional:
5a newspaper surveys:
— planning a questionnaire and presenting the findings
— pie chart
5a writing headlines
5a summary: the bare facts of a news story
5a-e writing a newspaper report
5a-e writing a balanced newspaper report by combining the viewpoints and facts from two news stories
5a-e sensationalised reports:
— of everyday events
— from given headlines
5a-e writing a balanced report after close examination of two biased reports and their source material
5a-e selecting and presenting news items as a newspaper for a known audience
5a-e planning and writing a school newspaper
5a-e using a diagram to explain how a prompting device works

5a-e letter expressing point of view about TV programme

5a-e TV viewing survey:
— designing a questionnaire
— presenting results in a variety of ways

5a-e own TV advertisement:
— writing for audience
— planning advertisement
— writing script
— preparing story board
— jingles and slogans
— recording the advert
— evaluating results

5a-e own chocolate bar:
— designing market research questionnaire
— designing chocolate bar
— designing wrapper
— market testing and recording
— advertising bar
— writing for audience

Cloze passage:

The actual words from the passage are given here for reference purposes only. They should not be regarded as the 'correct' answers.

1) win 2) the 3) is 4) me 5) a 6) the
7) If 8) you 9) give 10) While 11) this
12) dial 13) telephone 14) revolve
15) audience 16) breath 17) home
18) phone 19) ring 20) seconds 21) Then
22) someone 23) voice 24) speaking

Activity sheets:

5.3a group prediction *Fugitive* — 1 **AT1/5b; AT2/5b**

5.3b group prediction *Fugitive* — 2 **AT1/5b; AT2/5b**

5.3c group prediction *Fugitive* — 3 **AT1/5b; AT2/5b**

5.3d group prediction *Fugitive* — 4 **AT1/5b; AT2/5b**

5.3e modelling: hierarchies **AT3/5a**

5.3f skillmaster: search reading **AT2/5d**

5.3g skillmaster: direct and reported speech — 1 **AT3/5a**

5.3h skillmaster: direct and reported speech — 2 **AT3/5a**

5.3i close examination of text: *The Daily Record* **AT2/5b-c**

5.3j close examination of text: *The Wessex Observer* **AT2/5b-c**

5.3k News Editor: 1: news items

5.3l News Editor: 2: news items

5.3m listening skills: News Room — 1: selection/main idea **AT3/5a**

5.3n listening skills: News Room — 2: listening for detail/making notes **AT3/5a**

5.3o designing packaging/creating an advertisement **AT3/5a**

5.3p advertisement evaluation sheet **AT2/5b-c; AT3/5a**

5.3q story board: TV advertisement/ programme planning sheet **AT2/5a**

5.3r recipes for biscuit bases **AT2/5d**

5.3s recipes for fillings and toppings **AT2/5d**

5.3t packaging ideas **AT2/5d**

5.3u listening skills: following arguments/selecting suitable music for an advertisement **AT2/5a-b; AT3/5c-e**

Listening skills:

'News' and 'The Blind Men and the Elephant': appreciation/points of view/fact and opinion. **AT2/5b**
Side 1, track 5. Tape counter _____

There is no corresponding activity sheet for this track. It is the stimulus for *Reporting* on pages 38-9 in the pupil's book, and features a traditional story retold as 'News' by Aidan Chambers, and the poem 'The Blind Men and the Elephant' by John Godfrey Saxe.

NEWS

A rich landowner was returning home from a journey when he met by the side of the road the steward he had left in charge of his estate while he was away.

'Ah, steward,' hailed the returning gentleman cheerily, 'how are you, old fellow? And how are things at home?'

'Bad enough, sir,' said the steward. 'The magpie is dead.'

'Well, well,' said the gentleman. 'Poor magpie. Gone at last, eh? And how did he die?'

'Over-ate himself, sir.'

'Did he indeed! The greedy bird! What was it he liked so much?

'Horseflesh. That's what got him, sir. Horseflesh.'

'Never!' said the landowner. 'How ever did he manage to find so much horseflesh that it killed him?'

'All your father's horses, sir.'

'What! My father's horses! Are they dead too?'

'Aye, sir. Died of overwork.'

'Why ever should they be overworked, steward?'

'Carrying all that water, sir.'

'Carrying water! What were they carrying water for, man?'

'For sure, sir, to put the fire out.'

'Fire! What fire?'

'Why, sir, the fire that burned your father's house to the ground.'

'Good Lord, steward, is my father's house burnt down? How did that happen?'

'I reckon it was the torches, sir.'

'What torches?'

'Them we used at your mother's funeral, sir.'

'My mother is dead?'

'Aye, poor lady. She never looked up after it.'

'After what, man, after what?'

'The loss of your father, sir.'

'My father? Dead too?'

'Yes, poor gentleman. Took to his bed as soon as he heard of it.'

'Heard of what?'

'Of the bad news, sir.'

'More bad news! What bad news?'

'Well, sir, your bank has failed and all your money is lost, and you're not worth a penny in the world, sir. I thought I'd come and wait on you to tell you about it, sir, for I thought you'd like to hear the news.'

(Aidan Chambers)

THE BLIND MEN AND THE ELEPHANT

It was six men of Hindostan,
    To learning much inclined,
Who went to see the Elephant
    (Though all of them were blind):
That each by observation
    Might satisfy his mind.

The *first* approached the Elephant,
    And happening to fall
Against his broad and sturdy side,
    At once began to bawl:
"Bless me, it seems the Elephant
    Is very like a wall."

The *second,* feeling of his tusk,
    Cried, "Ho! what have we here
So very round and smooth and sharp?
    To me 'tis mighty clear
This wonder of an Elephant
    Is very like a spear."

The *third* approached the animal,
    And happening to take
The squirming trunk within his hands,
    Then boldly up and spake:
"I see," quoth he, "the Elephant
    Is very like a snake."

The *fourth* stretched out his eager hand
    And felt about the knee,
"What most this mighty beast is like
    Is mighty plain;" quoth he;
"'Tis clear enough the Elephant
    Is very like a tree."

The *fifth* who chanced to touch the ear
    Said, "Even the blindest man
Can tell what this resembles most;
    Deny the fact who can,
This marvel of an Elephant
    Is very like a fan."

The *sixth* no sooner had begun
    About the beast to grope,
Than, seizing on the swinging tail
    That fell within his scope,
"I see," cried he, "the Elephant
    Is very like a rope."

And so these men of Hindostan
    Disputed loud and long,
Each in his own opinion
    Exceeding stiff and strong,
Though *each* was *partly* in the right
    And all were in the wrong.

(John Godfrey Saxe)

5.3m & 5.3n 'News Room': telephone calls/interview/commentary: selection/main idea/listening for details/making notes **AT3/5a**
Side 1, track 6. Tape counter _____
The setting for this track is a busy newsroom. Stories come in by phone, and from a tape-recorded interview. Here is the dialogue heard on the cassette.

(Telephone rings)
Kath: Hello, news room.
Mr. Dawson: I'm ringing about that bad smell in Smith Street.
Kath: Could I have your name please?
Mr. Dawson: John Dawson.
Kath: Thank you Mr. Dawson, and where are you ringing from?
Mr. Dawson: From Smith Street, just round the corner from your office.
Kath: Oh, I see. You're ringing about the report we featured in yesterday's edition?
Mr. Dawson: Yes, you reported that the Gas Board has declared the area safe, but there's still a terrible smell near the junction with Wellington Street. Perhaps you could put that in tomorrow's paper?
Kath: Thank you Mr. Dawson, I've made a note of it. Thank you for calling.

(Telephone rings)

Kath: Hello, news room.

Ken: Hi, Gorgeous. It's your favourite ace reporter Ken Johnson here.

Kath: Just get on with it, Ken.

Ken: There's been a pile-up on the M62. A tanker carrying hydrochloric acid has collided with an articulated lorry between junctions 6 and 7. Acid has poured out of the tanker and the lorry has jack-knifed. The following traffic was travelling far too fast, resulting in a sixteen vehicle pile-up. Firemen are attempting to cut the survivors out, but some cars are so badly crushed that it is unlikely anyone has survived.

The westbound carriageway is completely blocked. I'll get back to you with more details as soon as I can.

Kath: Thanks for the report, Ken.

Phil: Kath, have you got that tape of the interview with Professor Hartley?

Kath: It's right here, Phil.

Phil: Thanks. Is this a spare cassette player?

Kath: Yes. Be my guest.

Phil: Thanks again.

(The tape is played:)

Kirsty: This is Kirsty Mathieson interviewing Professor Desmond Hartley at Green Forest Research Laboratories.

Professor, you seem to have made a most remarkable discovery. Could you tell us what it all means?

Hartley: Yes, Kirsty. As you know I have spent the last twenty years studying the ageing process, both in animals and human beings. It has long been the dream of man to live, if not forever, then considerably more than the three score years and ten which the Bible allows us.

I have now discovered a substance which is able to slow down the ageing process in rats so that they live twice as long. I am now looking for volunteers to try this substance on human beings.

Kirsty: What effect do you think it will have on people?

Hartley: There have been no side effects at all on rats, yet it remains to be seen if there will be any in man. If my substance has a similar effect to that on rats I should expect a person to remain with the body of a twenty-five year old for a further seventy years before ageing slowly over the remaining fifty or sixty years.

Kirsty: So that would give a person a lifespan of . . .

Hartley: 140 to 150 years. Possibly more!

Kirsty: What is this magic substance?

Hartley: That, of course, is a closely guarded secret!

Kirsty: When will we be able to buy it?

Hartley: Not for at least ten years, and then it will only be of use to people under 25.

Kirsty: Why is that?

Hartley: Because once normal ageing has begun my substance has little effect, but anyone under 25 will receive the full benefits.

Kirsty: So that means anyone under fifteen years old now could live to be 150?

Hartley: If we can perfect our drug in time, yes.

Kirsty: I wonder what children under 15 will think of living so long?

Hartley: It would be interesting to find out. Perhaps you could conduct such a survey for your article?

Kirsty: Thank you, Professor Hartley, I shall. Your magic substance could change the world!

Hartley: I very much hope it will.

Phil: That's unbelievable, Kath! Do you think Hartley is a crank?

Kath: He's been a highly respected scientist for thirty years, so I'm ready to believe him. Pity I'm too old to benefit.

(Telephone rings)

Kath: Hello, news room.

Male voice (urgent): There's been an explosion at the junction of Smith St. and Wellington St. Several people have been injured and the corner off-licence has been completely demolished. There are flames a good twenty feet high. Get a reporter out here quick!

Kath: And your name is . . ? Hello? Hello? He's rung up.

Kath: Phil, get out to the corner of Smith St. and Wellington as fast as you can. Seems like that horrible smell you wrote about yesterday has caused an explosion!

Phil: I'm on my way.

Kath: News room. Can I help you?

Hodgson: 'Odgson from 'Arrogate 'ere. I've got a peach of a story for you. There's been a strange creature sighted near Pately

Bridge. No one's 'ad a proper look at it, the blighter's too quick, but 'e savages sheep. Some folks say it's a great big dog. Are you getting all this, love?

Kath: Yes, Mr. Hodgson, I'm getting it all.

Hodgson: There's been two descriptions. Farmer Bates reckons it were like a giant cat, a panther or something. It left great paw prints, and two dead sheep.

Andy Armitage, a local lad, says it were dark brown with a couple of light patches on it. 'E thinks it were more like a dog, but 'e's not sure.

Kath: Were any people attacked?

Hodgson: No, 'e keeps away from people if 'e can. Killed seven sheep and an Alsatian.

Do I get my usual fee for tipping you off? I'm a bit short like.

Kath: Thank you, Mr. Hodgson, if we decide to follow up your story there'll be a cheque in the post. Thanks for ringing. 'Bye.

(Telephone rings again)

Kath: News room.

Phil: It's Phil Palmer, Kath. I'm in the phone box near the junction of Smith St. and Wellington. I can see everything here as it happens. Get your tape running for a live commentary!

Kath: Go ahead, Phil.

Phil: Walker's Off-Licence is completely wrecked. There was an explosion inside the shop five minutes ago. The front of the shop was blown out into the street and the inside of the building has collapsed.

Firemen are trying to put out a raging fire which has spread from the corner into both Smith Street and Wellington St. All houses in the area are being evacuated. There's rubble everywhere, and several cars have been damaged. One which had been parked outside Walker's is now upside down on the opposite side of the street. I've been told it belongs to the Walkers', but there's no sign of them. Police fear they are somewhere under the rubble of the shop. Firemen will start loooking for survivors when they have the fire sufficiently under control.

Another ambulance has now arrived. There are quite a number of injured and dazed people. Some of the more badly injured have already been taken to hospital, thanks to the efficiency of the ambulance service.

When I arrived here I spoke to a Mrs. Curtis who lives across the road from the off licence. The explosion blew her windows in,

but fortunately for her she was in the kitchen at the back. She ran into the front in time to see the shop collapse. Then flames began to engulf what was left of it.

Those flames are now out, and the other fires are being brought under control.

Mrs. Curtis believes the explosion was a gas leak. She said, "There has been a smell around this corner for days now. It must have been a gas leak, whatever they tell us." The police are busy evacuating the area in case of a further explosion. I shall have to leave this call box now. Send someone to collect the photographs I've taken.

Kath: I'll send Vicky out immediately. Thanks, Phil. See you soon.

The pupil's first task is to log each call by recording details such as the tape counter number, the time of the call (i.e. the main idea). Sheet **5.3m** should be used to record these details.

Sheet **5.3n** asks standard questions so that a summary of each news item can be made. Please note that there is not always sufficient information available to answer every question, but a summary of known facts is to be aimed for. The relatively uninteresting story of the bad smell on Smith St. develops during three reports into an explosion and resulting fire. Each separate Smith St. report should be summarised, with the final summary containing all the known information to date.

The tape and the completed activity sheets should then be used, together with activity sheets **5.3k** and **5.3l**, as the 'News Editor' assignment.

'News Editor' Assignment

This assignment begins on page 44 of the pupil's book, but also includes material on activity sheets **5.3k-5.3n** and on side 1, track 6 of the listening skills cassette.

The children should be split into three groups. Each group is the editorial team of a different newspaper: *The Daily Echo*, *The Morning Post* and *The Young Reporter*. Each newspaper has its own distinctive audience as explained in the pupil's book.

The editorial teams have to select news items from those printed on sheets **5.3k** and **5.3l**, and those to be heard on the cassette. (See previous notes). They should choose at least six items which they judge to be of interest to their audience and present them according to their newspaper's guidelines, which are given in the pupil's book. There are also editor's suggestions for each item on sheets **5.3k** and **5.3l**. Sheets **5.3m** and **5.3n** will help the groups to evaluate the items on the cassette.

The writing and artwork tasks should be shared out amongst the team. Extra details should be invented to make each story more interesting e.g. made up interviews, further developments, new facts etc. These should however be consistent with the original reports. 'Photographs', diagrams, maps, etc. may be included where appropriate. Other material such as cartoons, readers' letters, crosswords, advertisements, etc. may be added according to the group's interests and abilities.

After publication hold a discussion of the different approaches to the news stories. Ask each group why it chose the stories it did, and how the lead story was selected.

Have each group comment on the layout of the three papers. Discuss differences and similarities. How effective are the headlines? Compare headlines, content and style where the same story is featured. How have the stories been slanted for their different audiences? How successful do the teams think their edition has been? How might it be improved?

5.3u Following arguments/selecting suitable music for an advertisement
AT2/5a-b; AT3/5c-e
Side 2, track 1.   Tape counter _____
The track features part of a planning meeting at an advertising agency where music is being selected to feature in an advertisement for 'Swoop', a new chocolate biscuit. (See pages 56-7 in the pupil's book.)

The children have to listen to the music and what is said about it. They are first asked to give their own opinion about each piece of music, and then, taking into account the opinions expressed at the meeting, they are invited to select the music they consider to be most suitable.

As follow up work they are given the task of writing a one minute script for a TV advert.

Speaking/listening:
1 *Newspapers and Magazines*
AT1/5a, b & d
Discuss the differences between a newspaper and a magazine. Why do some newspapers have a colour magazine? How are such magazines different from ordinary magazines?

Make a collection of different magazines. Ask the children to choose one, read it and tell the class about it. Points to look at include the audience it is aimed at, its presentation (colour? photographs? attractive layout?, etc.), its information and entertainment content and its advertisements. The children should say why they liked or didn't like it.

2 *The History of Newspapers* **AT1/5a-d; AT2/5d**
Find out about the history of newspapers, including how news was made known before newspapers. Prepare a taped radio programme telling the story of newspapers. Include dramatised scenes and sound effects.

3 *The Future of Newspapers*
AT1/5a, b & d
Today newspapers compete with radio and television. What does the group think will happen to newspapers in the future? Will home printers connected to cable automatically print out newspapers for us, or will the printed word become less and less important?

Conduct a debate on a motion such as, 'This house believes there will soon be no need to have newspapers.'

4 *Opinion Poll* **AT1/5a, c & d**
Conduct an opinion poll on an issue of general interest. Plan a series of questions which will help you find out what people think. Record their views on tape and use the recording as a basis for a newspaper report.

5 *Radio/TV Interviews* **AT1/5b & d**
Divide the class into groups of about 6-10. One person in each group takes the role of radio/TV interviewer. A subject is then chosen such as the quality of school dinners, or the latest pop sensation, and the interviewer walks amongst the group asking their opinions. Record the interviews for replay later.

6 *Radio Phone-in Programme*
AT1/5b & d
Make and record a radio phone-in with members of the group expressing opinions on an issue of the moment.

7 *TV Cliches* **AT1/5a**
Write down three or four TV cliches, such as, 'We'll be right back after the break' or 'Conrad Splodge, Six O'Clock News, Calcutta'. Ask the group to listen out for these and their variations during an evening's viewing, and to make a note of their frequency.

8 *Quiz Shows* **AT1/5a & b**
Try your own versions of radio and TV quiz shows such as, 'Animal, Vegetable and Mineral', 'Twenty Questions', 'Any Questions', etc.

9 *Your Own TV Quiz Show* **AT1/5a & b**
Let the group devise their own TV quiz or game show. Record it on video tape.

10 *Complaints* **AT1/5a, b & c**
Act out scenes in which a customer returns a faulty item to a shop. Try a mixture of different customers and shop assistants: apologetic, angry, etc.

11 *Persuasion* **AT1/5a & b**
Discuss how the children set about trying to influence other people. Do they approach adults differently from children? Are different techniques required for older and younger children?

12 *Market Trader* **AT1/5a & b**
Let the group act out a scene where a market trader is trying to sell his various wares.

13 *Colour in Advertising* **AT1/5a & b**
Discuss the importance of colour in advertising and packaging. What do different colours suggest to the group? Which colours would be appropriate for some products, yet unsuitable for others?

14 *TV Advertisements* **AT1/5a, b & d**
Follow up the evaluation of the TV adverts by discussing how people are represented in the adverts. Are these people like anyone the group knows? Are the situations real?
  Can they explain why particular images were used?
  Which words are currently fashionable in advertisements?

15 *Market Research* **AT1/5a & b**
Discuss the function of market research. Is it worthwhile? Is it reliable? Have pupils ever been stopped by market researchers, or had them call at their house?

16 *Chocolate Snack* **AT1/5a, b & d**
Discuss the ingredients of the snack biscuit the group has designed. Does the snack have to contain chocolate? Is chocolate a good thing to eat? Would snack bars be as tasty without chocolate?
  Can the group tell the difference between real chocolate and chocolate flavoured coating? Which do they prefer? Are they prepared to pay more for real chocolate?

Follow-up work:

1 *Newspapers* **AT2/5c**
Ask the children to bring in old newspapers. Try to obtain examples of as many kinds as possible. The collection may then be used for a wide range of activities.

2 *Parts of a Newspaper* **AT2/5c**
Collect examples of various kinds of headline e.g. amusing/alliterative/tragic, etc. Find examples of reviews, cartoons, editorials, etc.

3 *Audience* **AT2/5c**
Select a number of different types of newspaper. Ask the group to try to say who they think the newspaper is aimed at. A close look at the adverts will be helpful here.
  If the same story is covered in different papers, ask the group how its presentation is changed to suit its assumed readers.

4 *Comparing Newspapers* **AT2/5c**
The children will spot obvious differences between the various papers, but ask them to look closely at such things as layout, content, reporting style, the use of photographs, cartoons and advertisements.

5 *Local Newspapers* **AT2/5c**
In what ways is a local newspaper different from a national paper?

6 *Fact and Opinion* **AT2/5c**
Give out suitable news stories. Ask the children to list the facts of each story, and any opinions they find. Invite them to express their own views about the article.

7 *Biased Reports* **AT2/5c**
Pages 42-3 feature two biased news reports, which are reprinted on activity sheets **5.3i** and **5.3j** to allow a closer study of the text. The questions are there to encourage an examination and discussion of the ways stories can be slanted.
Look for examples of the following:
— a careful choice of words or phrases to influence the reader
— omission of facts
— inclusion of facts which, although irrelevant, influence the way we see other facts
— slight alteration of the actual words of those interviewed
— omission of important words or statements from interviews
— reporting words out of context
Follow up this work by giving the group two or more versions of the same news story, and examining the stories for bias.
Ask questions along these lines:
Do the reports appear to be about the same events?
Do the reports contain the same facts?
Are there any contradictions in the reports?
Are any important facts left out? Why do you think this is?
What impression will a reader get from these reports?

8 *Poems from News Items* **AT3/5a & b**
Roger McGough's poem 'Rabbit in Mixer Survives' from *Waving at Trains* (Jonathan Cape) shows how a newspaper article can be turned into a poem. Most of the news cuttings on pages 36-37 in the pupil's book are suitable for such treatment. They give scope for humour (the girl in a jam), tall tales (the dog-eating pike), monsters (the lizardman), tragedy (the capsized steamer), cautionary tales (chewing pen tops), etc.

9 *Direct and Reported Speech* **AT3/5e**
Change the direct speech of cartoons into reported speech.
Record short interviews and conversations on tape. Write them in direct or reported speech. Rewrite newspaper articles changing all direct speech to reported speech, and vice versa.

10 *Writing to a Newspaper* **AT3/5a & b**
Find suitable newspaper letters and advertisements for the group to write replies to.

11 *Letterbox* **AT3/5a & b**
Make a noticeboard available and caption it "Letterbox". Let the children know that the board is for the expression of their ideas and opinions. The children may write anonymously if they wish, but it is perhaps wiser to have the letters delivered to the teacher rather than being pinned directly on the board!
A letter about TV programmes, local issues, or the provision of leisure facilities, etc. will probably be sufficient to stimulate further letters showing other points of view. Constructive criticism should be encouraged. New subjects may be introduced as children feel the need to express their feelings.

12 *A Class Newspaper* **AT2/5d; AT3/5a-e; AT4/5a-c**
There are a number of computer programs available which help in the preparation and printing out of newspaper pages. These are of varying complexity. The more expensive ones are more flexible, but they take a great deal of time to master. In practice the simpler, the better. Indeed a simple word processor like 'Folio' is just as suitable if the technique of 'cut and stick' is used.
Using this approach the articles are typed up and printed out using the smallest type setting, and headlines are then added using a larger typeface. These are then cut up, and various layouts of the finished page may be experimented with. If a more urgent report comes along before the paper is finished the page can then be reset. When the page layout is complete the articles are simply pasted into position. Copies may then be made by photocoping. If a single sheet is to be displayed then the page may be made as large as a real newspaper.

13 *Your Own Entertainment Magazine* **AT3/5a-e; AT4/5-5a-e**
Write an entertainments magazine with news, views and reviews of TV, radio, records, books, etc.

14 *Propaganda* **AT1/5a & b**
What is propaganda? Is it necessarily

wrong? Can there be such a thing as good propaganda? Stress the importance of trying to see all sides of an issue before making up one's mind.

15 *TV Camera Effects* **AT1/5a & b**
Record TV programmes and adverts to discuss the use of camera angles, zooming, panning (horizontal movement of the camera), tilting (vertical movement of the camera), tracking (moving the camera nearer to or further from the subject), crane shots (camera rising or falling vertically), fades and dissolves, slow and fast motion, etc.

Discuss the use of lighting to heighten effects.

Advertisements are generally more useful for such studies as they feature a greater range of effects than most programmes and have the added advantage of being short.

16 *Advertising and Packaging* **AT1/5b**
Collect advertisements from magazines and newspapers. Notice how colour is used, how important photographs are, what slogans are featured, etc.

Collect wrappers from snack bars and other products. Not only will these provide ideas for logos, slogans and packaging, but if randomly arranged on a plain background they will provide an attractive display.

Make a collection of junk mail. How many offer free samples, money-off coupons or introductory offers? How many are free competition entries or announcements of having 'won' prizes? How do people react to junk mail?

17 *Tasting Snack Bars* **AT1/5a & b**
How many children can recognise their favourite snack bar by taste alone? Collect together five or six similar snack bars. Allow blindfolded children to try to identify them. Can they explain what makes some snack bars distinctive?

Does the wrapper help in any way towards their enjoyment of the bar?

18 *McGinty's Gold*
This is the sixth *Adventures in English* program from Collins Educational. Placing the pupil in the role of a trainee reporter, it provides an ideal follow up to this unit.

The 28-page Pressure-fax book contains material for a study of newspapers, and a worksheet with helpful hints on the preparation of a school newspaper.

Full details of *McGinty's Gold* and the rest of the series are given in the appendices.

Name _____

ENGLISH
ALIVE

Level 5
Master

5.3a

Fugitive: Part 1

The small boy sat at the edge of the village, pushing the soft dust into little heaps and bombarding them with pebbles. With each puff of rising dust he imitated the sound of an explosion.

When he was bored with this game he looked around him. It was then he noticed a movement in the grass a short distance away. The movement ceased and after a few moments the boy returned to his game, but kept one eye on the grass.

Soon the grass was disturbed again. He raised a pebble and threw it into the grass. When this produced no result he began to hurl pebble after pebble.

Suddenly out of the grass rose a man in torn and dusty clothes. He ran in zig-zag movements away from the village, and the boy cried out in excitement. His mother came running, just in time to see the man dive out of sight into a dip in the ground. She gave an urgent shout and was soon joined by other villagers, but the man was not seen again.

To think and talk about

1   What do you think is happening? Who might the fugitive be?

2   What do you think will happen next?

5.3a Group prediction — 1
© 1990 Collins Educational
AT1/5b; AT2/5b

Name _____

ENGLISH
ALIVE

Level 5
Master

5.3b

Fugitive: Part 2

He lay completely motionless in the cold blackness. Fighting rising panic, he forced himself to breathe regularly. He concentrated entirely on blowing and sucking in a slow, regular rhythm. Gradually he became more relaxed.

He determined to ignore the creeping cold and the unknown creatures which explored such a strange intruder in their territory. Sometimes one of them nibbled at him. He longed to brush it away, but the least movement might prove fatal. He endured their explorations, hoping that nothing dangerous would take an interest in him.

Suddenly lights exploded in glittering, flowing patterns just above his upturned face. He carefully swallowed to ease a tickle in his throat, and lay as still as a rock. Slowly the lights grew less bright and disappeared. Still he lay there, though his muscles cried out for relief from the cold stiffness which gripped them. He counted slowly to two hundred, and then began all over again.

To think and talk about

1   What do you think is happening here?
    Where do you think the man is?
    Can you give any evidence to support your answer?

2   What do you think the lights are?

3   Why is the man counting?

4   What do you think will happen next?

5.3b Group prediction — 2
© 1990 Collins Educational
AT1/5b; AT2/5b

Name _____

ENGLISH
ALIVE

Level 5
Master

5.3c

Fugitive: Part 3

He was now sure he had crossed the border safely and was standing on friendly soil. He looked around for a road or sign of habitation. The landscape was completely empty except for an outcrop of rock some distance away. He set off towards it intending to use it as a lookout point. His pace quickened and the early morning sun began to take the stiffness out of his legs.

The guard on the rock was relaxing, soaking in the sun. When he became aware of the man's approach, he carefully shifted position, and slid silently down into the long grass, his camouflage hiding him completely. There he lay, perfectly still. He would let the man go past him, but if there was the least threat to him he would strike to kill.

The man's attention was fixed on the rocks. He had no suspicion of impending danger, and when his attacker struck he fell forward in bewilderment. The sharp pain knifed through his leg. He squirmed round to look at it. When he saw the wound he gasped in horror.

To think and talk about

1 Do you think the fugutive really is in friendly territory?
   What makes you think so?

2 Does his attacker puzzle you in any way?

3 Why do you think the fugutive is so horrified at his wound?

4 What do you think will happen to him now?

5.3c Group prediction — 3
© 1990 Collins Educational
AT1/5b; AT2/5b

Name _____

ENGLISH
ALIVE

Level 5
Master

5.3d

Fugitive: Part 4

The soldiers in the Land Rover saw the man waving to them feebly. The vehicle bounced over the rough ground and came to a stop in a cloud of dust.

"He's in a bad way!" he heard one of them say, and then he passed out.

*   *   *   *

James Miller, the Agadan correspondent for *The Daily News*, was sitting up in a hospital bed and feeling much better. He had already phoned his London office with a report on the rebel uprising in Agadan.

Now he was writing a few notes about his escape from the rebels. He told of how he had been seen by rebel villagers, and later chased by soldiers. He had hidden from them in the darkness by lying submerged in the shallows of a river, breathing through a hollow reed stem. They had searched for him with lights, which had glittered on the surface of the water just above his face. When they had gone he had swum silently across the river and hidden until dawn. At a lonely outcrop of rock he had been bitten by a poisonous snake. As he lay there dying he had been found and taken to hospital by two soldiers.

He put down his pen and closed his eyes. One day he would tell the full story in a book.

To think and talk about

1   Now you know who the man is, and what happened to him, read the story again.
    Which clues might have helped you decide what was going on?
        How did the author try to keep you guessing?
        How did he conceal the true identity of the guard on the rock?
        Which clues might have helped you guess?

2   Did you enjoy the story? Can you say why?
        Do you think the story woud have been more, or less, interesting if the author had not deliberately kept you guessing?

3   Discuss with your group what the story would read like if the author had told us all the facts as we went along. Record such a version on tape. Compare both versions.
        Which do you think works best? Can you say why?

5.3d   Group prediction — 4
© 1990 Collins Educational
AT1/5b; AT2/5b

Name _____

ENGLISH
ALIVE

Level 5
Master

5.3e

A Hierarchy Diagram

A hierarchy is a diagram which grades people in order of importance. It is shaped like a pyramid with the most important person at the top. Below him (or her) are those next in importance, and so on.

Look at this hierarchy diagram of the staff of Three Pines Primary School.

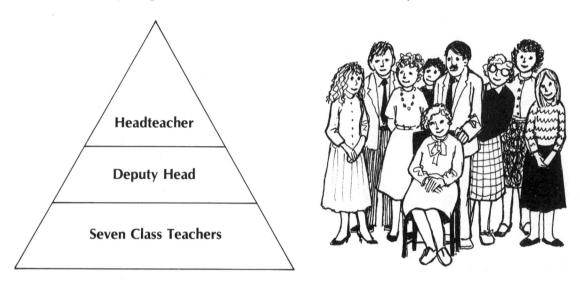

The Daily Fibber
Read this description of the editorial department of *The Daily Fibber*.

Conrad Massey is the editor of *The Daily Fibber*. Under him are specialist editors. Eddie Saxon is sports editor, Bill Green is political editor, and business is covered by John Unwin. Sally Gilham is arts editor, and Anthea Yarwood is features editor. They have seven assistant editors to help them. The rest of the department is made up of reporters, sub-editors and specialist writers.

1 Draw a hierarchy diagram of the organisation of *The Daily Fibber* editorial department.

2 Make your own hierarchy diagram of the organisation in your school.

Name _____

ENGLISH
ALIVE

Level 5
Master

5.3f

Search Reading

Turn to the newspaper reports on pages 36-7 in *English Alive — 5*. Use search reading to find the answers to the questions below.

Search reading means looking quickly for the information you need. This is how to do it.

> 1 Scan the headlines and topic sentences to find the correct report. The topic sentence tells us what the report is about. It is usually the first sentence in the report.
>
> 2 Skim through the report until you find the information you need.
>
> 3 Read that part of the report carefully.

1 Which school did the crime fighters attend? _____

_____

2 Where was the sleep-walking schoolboy travelling to? _____

_____

3 What was the exact location of the steamer disaster? _____

_____

4 What problems were caused by a computer breakdown? _____

_____

5 How many children die in Britain every year from inhaling a pen top? _____

_____

6 How big was the dog-eating pike? _____

7 Write a short description of the lizardman. _____

_____

_____

8 What reward is offered for its capture? _____

9 Name two other giant creatures mentioned in the article. _____

_____

10 How long did it take two girls to run from Mount Everest to Katmandu? _____

_____

The Daily Record

Read the interviews on pages 42-3 in Book 5 of *English Alive*. Then answer the questions below.

1. What effect does this word have on the reader?

2. Why do you think the reporter mentions these facts? What impression is he trying to give?

3. Why did the reporter use this word?

4. What is the reader expected to think about Northstar's plans when he reads this?

ANGRY DEMO AT NORTHSTAR SITE

There was an angry demonstration by local people yesterday at a Northstar drilling site in Wessex. It was the latest of several such demonstrations in Oakmead village during recent months.

TV producer, Martin Fitzpiers, a very recent Oakmead resident, took a leading role in the demonstration. Fitzpiers, whose current BBC TV series "Firepower" has been severely criticised for excessive violence, stated that the people of Oakmead would fight Northstar. "Actions speak louder than words," he warned. A reply by a spokesman for Northstar was lost in the chants of the crowd.

Northstar completed their oil explorations last May, and have since been awaiting the outcome of a series of meetings with the local people and the government. The Oakmead area has vast reserves of oil, which will be a tremendous boost to Britain's balance of payments, and create up to ninety new jobs. Northstar have already undertaken to restore the natural beauty of the area when the oil runs out in about ten years time.

Not all Oakmead residents object to Northstar's plans. Ms. Valerie Marshall told the Record she is happy to live in Oakmead. Alfred Melstock, a retired farm labourer, said he is looking forward to seeing the area re-landscaped.

East Wessex M.P. Nicholas Grantly also spoke at the demonstration. "I do appreciate the genuine concern of the local people," he said later. "That is why I have arranged a full debate on the Northstar project in the Oakmead village hall next Wednesday."

Grantly was confident that the community would come to see the advantages of Oakmead oil. After the demonstration he left Wessex for Downing Street to report the views of his constituents to the Prime Minister.

5. Did she really mean this?

6. Why did he say this?

7. What outcome does he want to see?

8. What do you think he will tell the P.M.?

5.3i Close examination
© 1990 Collins Educational
AT2/5b-c

The Wessex Observer

Read the interviews on pages 42-3 in Book 5 of *English Alive*. Then answer the questions below.

1. What effect does this word have on the reader?

2. Are these facts mentioned in the 'Daily Record' report?

3. Why are the words 'plummeting' and 'devastated' used?

4. What does this tell us about the opinion of the reporter?

5. What is the reader expected to think about Northstar when he reads this?

6. The 'Record's' report says 'Ms.' Why do you think this reporter uses 'Miss' instead?

7. Did she really ask this question?

8. How is this different from the 'Daily Record' report?

9. Whose side does Grantly appear to be on?

10. Why is this word used? What is its effect?

11. Is this fact or opinion?

OAKMEAD OIL PROTEST

The determined farmers and villagers of Oakmead held another (peaceful) demonstration against Northstar Oil today. They voiced their fears of lost farms, plummeting property values and a devastated environment.

Northstar are awaiting government approval to begin pumping oil in the Oakmead area. At least one farm will be lost if the project goes ahead. The (very real fear) of the local people is that one of the best loved beauty spots in the south of England will be ruined forever.

Northstar's claim that extensive landscaping would later restore the area, has to be seen against their record in Melset. Fountain Melbury, a once lovely valley, is still scarred two years after Northstar declared its landscaping programme a success.

Farmer William Stoke addressed the rally and explained how he would be forced to sell his family farm. "Northstar intend sinking their wells right in the middle of my land," he said sadly. "My family has lived here for three hundred years." He described the compensation offered by Northstar as a "sick joke."

(Miss) Valerie Marshall, a teacher at Oakmead Primary, warned of falling property values. "Who wants to live next to an oil well?" she asked.

The most famous Oakmead resident, TV producer Martin Fitzpiers, stressed the importance of the demonstration. "Actions speak louder than words," he said.

Nicholas Grantly, M.P., still appears to believe that the Oakmead community will give in to Northstar. He has arranged (yet) another talk by Northstar in Oakmead village hall on Wednesday next. Judging by the determination shown this afternoon he is in for a rude awakening.

Name_____

ENGLISH
ALIVE

Level 5
Master

5.3k

News Editor — 1

Before you begin this sheet please read page 44 in *English Alive* Book 5, which tells you how to use these news items. Further items can be found on sheet **5.3l** and on side 1, track 6 of Level 5 cassette.

```
o                                                            o
o   US Pop Star Karl Kane landed at Heathrow this            o
o   afternoon met by two thousand fans.                      o
o   Kane to play two concerts at Wembley Stadium             o
o   on Friday and Saturday next.                             o
o   Rumours of retirement from show biz at end of            o
o   year are still unconfirmed.                              o
o                                                            o
```

(Send a reporter to find out about his future plans.)

```
o                                                            o
o   An explosion at lunchtime damaged 'Glad Rags',           o
o   a boutique in the centre of Birmingham.                  o
o   Two people were taken to hospital suffering              o
o   from shock, but no injuries.                             o
o   Investigations into the cause continue.                  o
o                                                            o
```

(This is the third explosion in the area this month. Investigate!)

```
o                                                            o
o   Bristol school girl, Angela Thrift, 15, won             o
o   international art competition run by the                 o
o   Save Our Planet Project.                                 o
o   Her entry a painting of what life in Bristol            o
o   might be like in 2050.                                   o
o                                                            o
```

(We need a photo of the painting and an interview with the judges and Angela.)

```
o                                                            o
o   David, 12 son of well known financier Anthony            o
o   Yarnell has disappeared.  Last seen about a              o
o   mile from home near Matlock, Derbyshire, two            o
o   days ago.                                                o
o   Father offers substantial reward for                     o
o   information.                                              o
```

(We have a photograph of them both from a feature we did six months ago. Ring the father and ask for more information. Find out what the police are doing about it.)

```
o                                                            o
o   Reports of up to twenty UFOs from Saddleworth,           o
o   near Oldham.  Witness took photograph of one.           o
o   No comment from RAF.                                     o
o   A Manchester Airport radar operator claims to           o
o   have tracked five of them.                              o
o                                                            o
```

(We need that photograph. Talk to as many witnesses as you can. Get a quote from the radar operator.)

5.3k News Editor 1: news items
© 1990 Collins Educational

News Editor — 2

Before you begin this sheet please read page 44 in *English Alive* Book 5, which tells you how to use these news items. Further items can be found on sheet **5.3k** and on side 1, track 6 of Level 5 cassette.

```
Hurricane Frederick is now moving towards the
Bahamas after leaving 23 dead and thousands
homeless in Cuba.  Winds of up to 130 miles an
hour recorded as it swept across Cuba.
Widespread flooding and damage to buildings
and powerlines.  Havana severely hit.  Cuba cut
off from all outside contact.
State of emergency declared in the Bahamas.
Shops cleared of food and basic supplies in
panic buying.
```

(This story to have a map showing the path of the hurricane from its beginnings in the Caribbean, across Jamaica and Cuba towards the Bahamas, together with some background material on the nature of hurricanes.)

```
Belgian Grand Prix win for British driver
Paul Shaw in a Honda puts him 12 points ahead
of Angelo Frascati in world championship
ratings.  Second was Honda team mate, Andrew
Jarvie.  Frascati dropped out when his Ferrari
developed engine trouble.
```

(This makes Shaw almost unbeatable.)

```
Double decker bus crashed into electrical
shop in Hexham, Northumberland this lunchtime,
injuring two eight year old boys on the
pavement.  Driver suffered heart attack.  All
three comfortable in hospital.  No other
injuries, but extensive damage to bus and
shop front.
```

(See if we can get a photograph of this.)

```
The cat of Conservative MP Cosmo Tyrell,
which disappeared in move to new home in
Surbiton, has found its way back to old home
in Lincolnshire, some three weeks and 200
miles later.
```

(We need a photograph of the cat and a statement from Tyrell.)

```
Missing climber Dr. Garry Mansley, 29, found
today by search party.  Dr. Mansley disappeared
two days ago in a blizzard on Mount Everest.
He is said to be suffering from exposure.
```

(Try to find out more information.)

5.3l News Editor 2: news items
© 1990 Collins Educational

News Room — 1

Use this sheet to log the five telephone calls on side 1, track 6 of the Level 5 listening skills cassette.

1

Tape counter number _____

Time to call _____

Name of caller _____

Nature of call _____ Bad smell
_____ in Smith Street.
_____
_____

2

Tape counter number _____

Time to call _____

Name of caller _____

Nature of call _____

_____

_____

_____

3

Tape counter number _____

Time to call _____

Name of caller _____

Nature of call _____

_____

_____

_____

4

Tape counter number _____

Time to call _____

Name of caller _____

Nature of call _____

_____

_____

5

Tape counter number _____

Time to call _____

Name of caller _____

Nature of call _____

_____

_____

News Room — 2

Use this sheet to make notes for the first two news stories on Level 5 cassette: side 1, track 6.
Answer the questions, but remember that sometimes you are not given sufficient information to answer every question.

Copy the headings on a separate sheet and make notes on the remaining stories.

| Bad Smell in Smith Street |

Who did it? _____

Where did it happen? _____

When did it happen? _____

What happened? _____

_____

_____

Why did it happen? _____

_____

How did it end? _____

_____

| Accident on the M62 |

Who did it? _____

Where did it happen? _____

When did it happen? _____

What happened? _____

_____

_____

Why did it happen? _____

_____

How did it end? _____

_____

5.3n Listening skills — 2
© 1990 Collins Educational
AT3/5a

Name —————————————————

A New Breakfast Cereal

1 Think up a name for a new breakfast cereal.
2 Write a slogan for it.
3 Which colours would make a cheerful packet at breakfast time? Design an attractive carton in these colours and add the details to the cereal packet above. Include such things as the name of the product, the manufacturer's name, your slogan, and the ingredients.
4 Write a radio advertisement jingle for the cereal and record it on cassette.

5.30 Designing packaging/creating an advertisement
© 1990 Collins Educational
AT3/5a

Looking at TV Advertisements

Use this sheet to help you think about and
make notes on a TV advertisement.

Name of product _____

Features people/cartoon characters/computer graphics/puppets/other.

(Delete those not applicable). If other, please specify _____

What is the immediate appeal of the advert? _____

_____

What slogan or jingle is used? _____

_____

How important is colour in the advert? _____

_____

What audience is the advert aimed at? _____

What emotion (feeling) is aimed at? _____

How does the advertiser set out to achieve this? _____

_____

Does he succeed? _____

Other notes _____

5.3p Advertisement evaluation sheet
© 1990 Collins Educational
AT2/5b-c; AT3/5a

Name _____

Story Board Planning Sheet

Produced by: Title: Sheet number:

Frame no.	Frame no.

Information/words:

Frame no.	Frame no.

Frame no.	Frame no.

5.3q Story Board
© 1990 Collins Educational
AT2/5a

Name _____

Recipes for Biscuit Bases

These recipes and suggestions are in proportions suitable only for trials and testing. Increase the quantities equally for batch baking. The recipes may be used as they are or adapted. If you prefer, you may use your own recipes.

FLAPJACKS (an oatmeal biscuit)

25g	butter
10ml	golden syrup
15g	soft brown sugar
50g	rolled oats

Melt the butter, syrup and sugar in a pan over a very low heat. Stir in the oats. Spread the mixture on a greased baking sheet. Bake in a moderate over (160°C, Gas Mk 4) for 20 minutes until golden brown.

(Alternatives)
1. Add 10g dried fruit/coconut/chocolate chips/glacé cherries to mixture.
2. Use muesli breakfast mix instead of rolled oats.

SHORTBREAD (a plain, rich biscuit)

50g	plain flour
15g	semolina/ground rice
10g	caster sugar
40g	butter

Put flour, sugar and rice in a bowl. Rub in the butter until a dough is formed. Shape this into a square 1cm thick. Bake in a moderate oven (160°C, Gas Mk 4) for 30 minutes, until firm and golden.

(Alternatives)
1. Add 10g dried fruit/cherries/chocolate chips or peanuts.
2. Flavour the shortbread with a few drops of orange essence.
3. Add 2 tspn cocoa to the flour to make chocolate-flavoured shortbread.

CRUMBLY BISCUIT

60g	digestive biscuits (crumbled up using a rolling pin)
30g	butter

Melt the butter slowly in a pan. Add the biscuits and press the mixture into a well-greased tray. Firm down with the back of a metal spoon. Chill for 30 minutes until firm.

(Alternatives)
1. use chocolate-covered digestives, bourbon biscuits or ginger biscuits for different flavours.
2. Add dried fruit or nuts.

CRISPIES

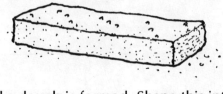

1 small block of cooking chocolate
Rice Crispies

Slowly melt the chocolate in a dish over a pan of water. Add the Rice Crispies and stir until they are covered. Press the mixture into a greased tray. Leave to set.

(Alternatives)
1. Use cornflakes, muesli or crushed biscuit crumbs instead of rice.
2. Add dried fruit or nuts.
3. Use white, dark or flavoured chocolate.

Other suggestions:
Use pre-bought biscuits, wafers etc. This can save time and trials, but remember to include the cost of your pre-bought biscuits when calculating your selling price.

5.3r Recipes for biscuit bases
© 1990 Collins Educational
AT2/5d

Name _____

ENGLISH
ALIVE

Level 5
Master

5.3s

Fillings and Toppings

These recipes and suggestions are in proportions suitable only for trials and testing. Increase the quantities equally for batch baking. The recipes may be used as they are or adapted. If you prefer, you may use your own recipes.

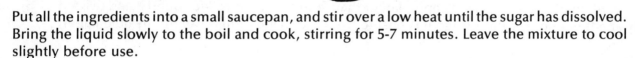

CREAMY CARAMEL

30g	butter
15g	caster sugar
10ml	golden syrup
50ml	condensed milk (tinned)

Put all the ingredients into a small saucepan, and stir over a low heat until the sugar has dissolved. Bring the liquid slowly to the boil and cook, stirring for 5-7 minutes. Leave the mixture to cool slightly before use.

(Alternatives)
1. Peanuts or hazelnuts, cherries or dried fruit may be added.
2. The caramel may be used as a topping or as a filling.

COCONUT ICE

100g	sugar
50g	butter
a few drops of lemon juice	
50g	desiccated coconut
30ml	milk

Dissolve the sugar gently in the milk over a low heat. Simmer gently stirring occasionally. Stir in the butter and remove from heat. Beat the mixture vigorously until it is very thick and creamy. Stir in the coconut and lemon. Beat well again before use.

(Alternatives)
1. If pink coconut ice is required, add a drop of food colouring.
2. Add drops of fruit flavouring e.g. orange/raspberry for a fruitier taste.

FUDGE FILLING

50g	sugar
30ml	water
30ml	condensed milk (tinned)
10g	soft margarine

Put the sugar and water in a pan and heat gently until the sugar dissolves. Add the condensed milk and bring to the boil. Continue to boil, stirring all the time, until a small sample, when dropped, forms a ball. Remove from the heat* and beat until creamy. Pour on to biscuit base.

(Alternatives)
1. Add 10g walnuts, peanuts or chopped fruit at * stage.
2. Melt 20g of chocolate and add at * stage.

CHOCOLATE COATING

There is a wide variety of different coloured and flavoured cooking chocolates available on the market. Different effects can be achieved if you mix these: swirling white and dark chocolate together can produce dramatic effects. Many things can be added to chocolate once it has been melted over water, but **never** add any liquids. Leave your biscuits to set on greaseproof paper.

Packaging

The packaging you select for your snack bar will depend on a number of things:

 a) the size and shape of your snack;
 b) the papers you have available;
 c) how you want your product to look.

Here are a few suggestions, but for more ideas see how your own favourite snacks are wrapped.

1   The Twist

This is very simple. A rectangle of paper, larger than your biscuit, is rolled round it and twisted firmly at either end. For this design it is best to use cellophane or lightweight, flexible paper.

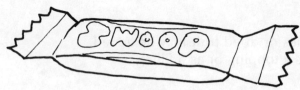

2   Roll and seal

This method too is fairly simple. Again a rectangle of paper is needed, but this time the edges are sealed with glue and then neatened off with pinking shears. The design is suitable for most types of paper.

3   Foil and Sheath

First wrap your snack bar carefully in foil. Then wrap around it a long paper sheath bearing the product's name and other information. This wrapper is particularly suitable for flat, smooth snacks.

4   Bundle

This is a very attractive wrapping and requires a large square or circle of cellophane or thin, flexible paper. The snack should be placed in the centre of the sheet and the edges should all be gathered up and tied with string or ribbon. This wrapper is suitable for small or irregular-shaped snack bars.

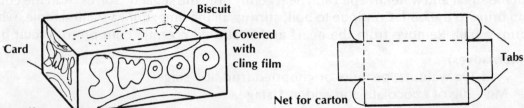

Biscuit

Card

Covered with cling film

Net for carton

Tabs

5   Carton and Cling Film

Work out a net that is suitable in size and depth for your biscuit. Cut it out of thick paper or card. Assemble it, and then cover the package with cling film.

General note

If you are using sugar paper or coloured printing papers for wrapping your snacks, it is advisable to pre-wrap them in greaseproof paper to prevent the colours spoiling.

5.3t Packaging suggestions
© 1990 Collins Educational
AT2/5d

Name_____

ENGLISH
ALIVE

Level 5
Master

5.3u

Swoop — the family's favourite

A Write *your* opinion of each piece of music.

1 _____

_____

2 _____

_____

3 _____

_____

4 _____

_____

B Taking into account the reactions of everyone at the meeting, which piece of music do you think would be most suitable for the 'Swoop' advertisement? Give reasons for your answer.

_____

_____

_____

_____

_____

_____

C Write a one minute script for a 'Swoop' TV advert. Remember it should have family appeal, and must include the slogan, 'Swoop — the family's favourite.'

5.3u Listening skills
© 1990 Collins Educational
AT2/5a-b; AT3/5c-e

Unit 4

Theme — The *Titanic*
Stimuli — account of tragedy with
          contemporary photographs
          Daily Mirror cutting, 14/4/1912
          Chicago Tribune cutting, same
          date
          photographs and passage from
          The Discovery of the Titanic by
          Robert D. Ballard, Hodder &
          Stoughton
          Sunday Times cutting, 3/11/1987
          Passage from *A Night to
          Remember,* Walter Lord,
          Penguin

AT1 Speaking/listening
5a-d conducting an inquiry into the
Titanic disaster, based on the material in
the book unit together with any additional
information available e.g. *A Night to
Remember* by Walter Lord, Penguin
5a — account of the disaster
5b — contribute to discussion
5c — convey information and ideas
effectively
5d — group presentation

AT2 Reading
The story of the *Titanic* disaster:
5b finding facts
5b finding reasons
5b looking for evidence
5b inference
5b projection
5b reading for the main idea
5b speculation
5b, d evaluation of survival figures
Contemporary newspaper reports:
5b speculation
5b-d checking facts
5b-d evaluation of newspaper articles
The discovery of the *Titanic*:
5b finding facts
5b finding reasons
5b, d evaluation
Research skills:
5d using an atlas to find location of the
Titanic wreck
5d finding out about wireless and
telegraph messages
5d finding out about other sea disasters

AT3 Writing
5a time line
5a listing factors which contributed to
the disaster
5a-e headlines and opening paragraphs
for newspaper report
5a-e the story of the disaster from the
viewpoint of a survivor

Activity sheets:
5.4a Modelling: Time line (links directly to
      information in the pupil's
      book) **AT3/5a**
5.4b Cloze procedure (see answer
      below) **AT2/5b**
5.4c Fact find: Famous Ships **AT2/5d**
5.4d Fact find: Picture search **AT2/5d**
5.4e Reference skills: Disasters **AT2/5d;**
      AT3/5a-d
5.4f Word search **ATs1-4**

Listening skills: AT2/5d; AT3/5a-d
5.4g Selection: listening for specific detail
Side 2, track 3 Tape counter _____
This track features an extract from *A Night
to Remember* by Walter Lord.
The pupil is asked to listen for the answers
to five questions:
1 What was the weather like on the night
  the *Titanic* struck the iceberg?
  (It was calm, clear and bitterly cold.)
2 How did the iceberg appear to the
  lookout?
  (Something directly ahead, even darker
  than darkness. At first it was the size of
  two tables put together, but it grew
  larger and closer by the second.)
3 What did the bump suggest to these
  passengers:
  a) Major Arthur Godfrey Peuchen? (A
     heavy wave striking the ship.)
  b) Mrs. J. Stuart White? (The ship
     seemed to roll over a thousand
     marbles.)
  c) Lady Cosmo Duff Gordon? (As
     though someone had drawn a giant
     finger along the side of the ship.)
4 How did other passengers know the
  truth?
  (Some saw the ice through a porthole.
  Another passenger saw chunks of ice
  falling through his open porthole.)
5 What happened in the boiler room?
  (The whole starboard side of the ship
  seemed to give way, and the sea
  cascaded in.)

Answer to the cloze passage (5.4b)

Any words which make sense are acceptable, but the actual words used by the author are given here for reference purposes.

1) books 2) of 3) Yet 4) fast 5) sank
6) life 7) many 8) *Titanic* 9) on
10) passengers 11) size 12) iceberg
13) spot 14) were 15) strangest 16) his
17) coincidences 18) fiction 19) sailing
20) seaman 21) began 22) on 23) day
24) eyes 25) but 26) build 27) close
28) sea 29) been 30) danger 31) halt
32) name

Background material:

The standard reference book on the Titanic disaster is Walter Lord's *A Night to Remember* (Penguin). The more recent *The Discovery of the Titanic* by Dr. Robert D. Ballard (Hodder and Stoughton) provides fascinating colour photographs of the wreck in 1986, together with excellent 1912 photographs, some of which have not been published before.

Contemporary newspaper accounts may be obtained from the British Library (Newspaper Library), Colindale Avenue, London NW9 5HE.

Follow up work:

1 *If only . . .* **AT3/5a**
A series of bizarre coincidences led to the tragedy. If only the ice warnings had been heeded . . . If only the lookouts had spotted the iceberg a few seconds earlier . . . If only there had been a moon that night . . . If only the *Titanic* had not been travelling so fast . . . If only the *Titanic* had had enough lifeboats . . . if only the *Californian* had come to her rescue . . . The group could probably add more.

Sort the list into those factors due to human error and those beyond control. Can any lessons be learned from all this?

2 *Communication* **AT2/5d**
How did the British newspapers come to get the story so completely wrong? (See the extract from *The Daily Mirror* in the book unit: 'Everyone Safe', 'Helpless Giant Being Towed to Port by Allan Liner', etc.) The answer to this must lie in the limited range of early radio (wireless) as opposed to the longer range of telegraph (using wires). Find out more about such communications in 1912.

Why do you think Captain Smith asked for a CQD emergency signal to be sent? CQD had been superseded by SOS on July 1st, 1908. The radio operators decided to use both CQD and SOS, the first time SOS had been sent at sea. What is the general distress call on radio equipment today? (Mayday, from the French *m'aidez.*)

3 *Local Newspapers* **AT1/5a & b; AT2/5d**
Try to obtain contemporary copies of local newspapers. How do they treat the story? Is it different from the national newspapers? Is there any local interest e.g. passengers, crew, seaport? Does this make the report more interesting?

4 *Recent Sea Disasters* **AT2/5d**
Compare the contemporary treatment of the *Titanic* disaster to the media treatment of more recent sea disasters such as the Zeebrugge ferry disaster, the *Herald of Free Enterprise.*

5 *Titanic Lost?* **AT1/5a, b & d**
Discuss how the *Titanic* disaster would be treated today. Prepare newspaper, radio and TV reports: interview survivors, relatives of those lost, representatives of the 'White Star Line' and the ship builders, Harland & Wolff; make sketches and paintings (to stand for photographs); obtain comments from experts as to how and why the tragedy happened, etc. *The Discovery of the Titanic* is useful here, as it sheds new light on the way the liner went down.

6 *International Memorial* **AT1/5a, b & d**
What are the views of the group about recent 'plundering' of the wreck? Do they think Dr. Ballard was right to leave all artefacts where they lay? Was the French expedition right to bring up objects from a site many people think should be left as an international memorial and grave?

Discuss how the group might feel if any of their relatives had been lost in the disaster.

Children are intrigued by the thought of skeletons, or even ghosts, on the wreck, but Ballard found no bodies: they had disappeared long ago. Several pairs of shoes lie on the seabed, however, probably where bodies came to rest.

Name _____

Time Line

Complete this time line with the events of the night the *Titanic* sank.

> *Sunday, April 14th to Monday, April 15th, 1912*

1.42pm — Warning received of icebergs 250 miles ahead of *Titanic*

5.50pm —

———— Three warning messages received from the *Californian*.

8.55pm —

9.30pm —

11.30pm —

———— Lookout sights iceberg.

2.18am —

3.30am —

↓ *Carpathia* ends her search for survivors.

5.4a Modelling
© 1990 Collins Educational
AT3/5a

The Sinking of the Titan

Think for yourself what the missing words are in this passage. Write *one* word in each space.

In 1898, on her maiden voyage, the biggest and most luxurious liner ever built struck an iceberg in the North Atlantic and sank, with appalling loss of life.

The story does not appear in history _____ because it happened only in the pages

_____ *Futility,* a novel by Morgan Robertson. _____ fourteen years

later fiction gave way to _____ when the *Titanic* struck an iceberg and

_____ on her maiden voyage, with heavy loss of _____.

The disaster in Robertson's novel has _____ other similarities with that of the

_____. In both cases the ships were on their way to America, carrying rich

_____. Both ships were roughly the same _____, and were

considered unsinkable. Both struck an _____ and sank in exactly the same

_____ in the Atlantic. In each case there _____ not enough lifeboats.

Yet perhaps the _____ coincidence is the name Robertson gave to

_____ ship: the *Titan.*

Strange though these _____ may be, truth is sometimes stranger than

_____. In April, 1935 a tramp steamer was _____ from Tyneside to

Canada. A young _____, William Reeves, was on watch. He _____ to

think about the *Titanic* disaster _____ April 14th, 1912. It was the _____

he had been born. He strained his _____ to catch any glimpse of danger,

_____ could see nothing. The coincidences began to _____ up in his

mind: the time was _____ to that of the Titanic disaster, and the _____

was as calm as it had _____ then. He panicked and shouted out a

_____ signal. The steamer came to a _____ — just metres away from a

huge iceberg. The _____ of that tramp steamer was yet another coincidence. It was

the *Titanian.*

Can you think of a better title for the passage? _____

Famous Ships

Use your reference library to complete this chart.

Famous Person	Name of Ship	Year	Event
Capt. Smith	Titanic	1912	Sank with enormous loss of life on maiden voyage.
Sir Francis Drake			Flagship of British fleet when Spanish Armada came.
Capt. Cook	Endeavour		Charted New Zealand coasts and visited Australia.
Capt. Cook		1772	
Scott	Discovery		First Antarctic expedition.
Scott		1910	
Shackleton		1914	
Columbus			
Amundsen	Fram		Discovered South Pole.

Vessels in Fiction

1 What is the name of Captain Nemo's submarine in Jules Verne's

   Twenty Thousand Leagues Under the Sea? _____

2 Which vessel appears in the title of a book by C. S. Lewis? _____

3 Which ship was wrecked at the beginning of R. M. Ballantyne's

   The Coral Island? _____

5.4c   Fact find
© 1990 Collins Educational
AT2/5d

Name _____

Picture Search

Can you name these boats and ships? Use your reference library to help you. Write the correct name under each one.

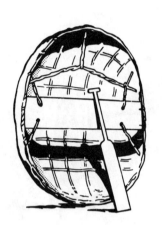

_____

_____

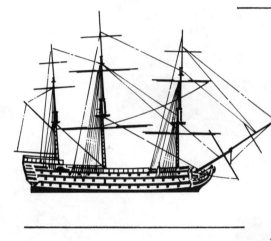

_____

_____

_____

_____

_____

Choose one of the above and write a paragraph about it.

5.4d   Fact find
© 1990 Collins Educational
AT2/5d

Disasters

Choose *one* of these disasters. Find out as much as you can about it from your reference library, and then write an account of it.

The Eruption of Krakatoa

The Hindenburg

The San Francisco Earthquake

The Space Shuttle Explosion

The Tay Bridge Disaster

Look for the answers to these questions.

Where did it happen?
When did it happen?
What happened?
Why did it happen?
How did it end?
What lessons were learned from the disaster?
Could it ever happen again?

The Great Fire of London

5.4e   Reference skills/writing
© 1990 Collins Educational
AT2/5d; AT3/5a–d

Nautical Word Search

These twenty words are hidden in the word search. Look for them horizontally, vertically and diagonally. Some are written backwards.

When you have found them all, choose *six* and put each one in a sentence to show its meaning.

schooner	
scuppers	
capstan	
sloop	
spinnaker	
halyard	
boom	
starboard	
derrick	
windlass	
davit	
prow	
sextant	
hull	
porthole	
stern	
trawler	
catamaran	
buoy	
keel	

s	a	h	u	l	l	w	i	n	c	s	p
j	l	c	a	t	a	m	a	r	a	n	y
p	e	f	m	l	h	g	c	e	p	e	v
o	e	t	h	q	y	w	d	t	s	b	u
r	k	x	d	o	o	a	d	s	t	o	z
t	t	b	u	r	i	t	r	u	a	o	e
h	n	b	p	d	a	b	g	d	n	m	w
o	a	s	c	h	o	o	n	e	r	d	i
l	t	i	v	b	f	o	b	r	l	a	n
e	x	s	n	q	u	m	d	r	g	v	d
r	e	l	w	a	r	t	b	i	a	i	l
j	s	l	o	o	p	w	s	c	k	t	a
t	o	s	p	i	n	n	a	k	e	r	s
p	m	v	p	s	c	u	p	p	e	r	s

_____
_____
_____
_____
_____
_____
_____

5.4f Nautical word search
© 1990 Collins Educational
ATs1-4

Name _____

The Titanic

1 What was the weather like on the night the *Titanic* struck the iceberg?

_____

_____

2 How did the iceberg appear to the lookout? _____

_____

3 What did the bump suggest to these passengers:

   a) Major Arthur Godfrey Peuchen? _____

_____

   b) Mrs. J. Stuart White? _____

_____

   c) Lady Cosmo Duff Gordon? _____

_____

4 How did other passengers know the truth? _____

_____

_____

5 What happened in the boiler room? _____

_____

_____

_____

Follow-up work
Use the information above to help you write an account of the *Titanic's* collision with the iceberg.

5.4g Listening skills
© 1990 Collins Educational
AT2/5d; AT3/5a–d

Unit 5

Theme — Changes
Stimuli — picture maps of the (fictional)
town of Chadwick
'Finders Keepers', Andrew
Moore, *Daily Telegraph*
'This letter's to say' — Raymond
Wilson, *A Fourth Poetry Book,*
Oxford
extract from Collins
Thesaurus
'Mad Meals' by Michael Rosen,
from *Quick Let's Get Out of
Here,* André Deutsch
from *Revolting Rhymes* by Roald
Dahl, Jonathan Cape
from *The Wrestling Princess* by
Judy Corbalis, André Deutsch

AT1 Speaking/listening
Public Inquiry:
5b — expressing viewpoint
5b — listening and responding to the
contributions of others
5b, c — preparing speech
5b, d — role play
5b discussion and evaluation of
traditional tales

ATs1-4 Word study
Anglo-Saxon place name origins
matching place names to meanings
new words:
old words with new meanings
compound words
borrowing from other languages
words and names
words from science
acronyms
slang
etymology
prefixes
palindromes
synonyms
antonyms
thesaurus
spoonerisms
malapropisms
idioms
double negatives
ambiguity
irony
past and future tense

AT2 Reading
5a preferences between two versions of
story
5b ambiguity
5b irony
5b inference
5b poem:
— reading for detail
— imaginative response
— evaluation
5b, d maps:
— using map and text to select a site for an
Anglo-Saxon farm
— scale — estimating and measuring
distances
— estimating travelling times
— reading for detail
— inference
— reasoning
— using the picture map to make a model
of the area
5b, d reading for detail/inference
5d dictionary
5d encyclopedia
5d thesaurus
5d newspaper report
5e awareness of author's choice of words

AT3 Writing
The writing process:
5b — sentence structure, punctuation
5b — ellipsis
5b — reported and direct speech
Poetic:
5a recipe
5a menu
5a-b, d found poem using various sources
5a-e description of busy street
5a-e explaining how a bypass would
change things
5a-e descriptive poem expressing
feelings
5a-e essay
5a-e list poem
5a-e nursery rhymes with a twist
5a-e traditional tale with a twist
5a-e narrative, writer as spectator
5a-e picture book for younger children
Transactional:
5a writing notes
5a-e letters of protest
5a-e recording changes in local district in
the form of a book with photographs
5a-e poster

AT4/5 Presentation
5a spelling
5b checking final drafts

Activity sheets:

5.5a modelling: graphs **AT3/5a**

5.5b listening skills: evaluating a speaker's attitude **AT2/5b-c**

5.5c fact find: encyclopedia **AT2/5d**

5.5d fact find: *Guinness Book of Records* **AT2/5d**

5.5e Americanisms **ATs1-4**

5.5f prefixes **AT4/5a; ATs1-4**

5.5g Skillmaster: future tense **ATs1-4**

5.5h group prediction: *The Emerald Necklace* — 1 **AT1/5b; AT2/5b**

5.5i group prediction: *The Emerald Necklace* — 2 **AT1/5b; AT2/5b**

5.5j group prediction: *The Emerald Necklace* — 3 **AT1/5b; AT2/5b**

5.5k group prediction: *The Emerald Necklace* — 4 **AT1/5b; AT2/5**

5.5l listening skills: evaluating a speaker's attitude/sex bias/prejudice **AT1/5b; AT2/5b**

Listening skills: AT2/5b-c

5.5b evaluating a speaker's attitude
Side 2, track 3. Tape counter _____

Two residents of Chadwick, the town featured in the pupil's book, are interviewed for television about the bypass. The pupil's task is to evaluate their attitudes and identify emotive words.

Science AT5/5c

Answers appear on the answer cards in the appendices.

5.5l evaluating a speaker's attitude/sex bias/prejudice **AT1/5b; AT2/5b**
Side 2, track 4. Tape counter _____

This track features a conversation between a man and a woman, old school friends, meeting in the street. The children should evaluate their arguments and their attitudes to the opposite sex. They should try to identify sex bias and prejudice and later examine these in group discussion.

As the questions are designed to encourage discussion, there is no answer card for this sheet.

Speaking/listening:

1 *Sex Equality and Stereotypes* **AT1/5a, b & d**
Discuss the roles of men and women in today's world. What changes have taken place over the last hundred years? Are more changes needed? Are men and women really equal? Are there any jobs which one sex will always be able to do better? Should these jobs be reserved for that sex only? What makes you think so?

Make a list of leisure activities enjoyed by the group. Are there any which are popular with only one sex? Why does the group think this is? Why shouldn't such activities be enjoyed by the other sex?

Discuss what is meant by stereotypes. Look for sex stereotypes in books, advertisements, television and films.

2 *Drama* **AT1/5a, b & d**
Dramatise scenes from myths and legend.

3 *Talking Books* **AT1/5a & b**
Record stories and/or dramatised extracts as talking books for the blind.

4 *Everyday Sayings* **AT1/5a & b**
Collect idioms, proverbs and other everyday sayings, and write them on card. Give them out at random to each member of the group. Each person in turn then explains the meaning of his saying to the rest of the group. Anyone failing to do so drops out and new cards are given to those remaining.

Alternatively the group may be split into smaller groups and each group given a card. The saying should be discussed by the group and a story made up to show its meaning. This story may then be dramatised. The other children should try to identify the saying from the story.

5 *English Spelling* **AT4/5-5a-c**
English spelling presents great difficulties to those attempting to learn the language. This poem will help the children to understand some of the problems they face.

Hints on Pronunciation For Foreigners
I take it you already know
Of tough and bough and cough and dough?
Others may stumble, but not you
On hiccough, thorough, laugh and through?
Well done! And now you wish perhaps
To learn of less familiar traps?
Beware of heard, a dreadful word
That looks like beard and sounds like bird.
And dead: it's said like bed, not bead —
For goodness sake don't call it 'deed'!
Watch out for meat and great and threat,
They rhyme with suite and straight and debt.

A moth is not a moth in mother
Nor both in bother, broth in brother
And here is not a match for there
Nor dear and fear for bear and pear,
And then there's dose and rose and lose—
Just look them up—and goose and choose.
And cork and work and card and ward,
And font and front and word and sword,
And do and go and thwart and cart —
Come, come, I've hardly made a start!
A dreadful language? Man alive,
I'd mastered it when I was five.
(by T.S.W.)

Make a collection of other words
whose spelling and pronunciation are
confusing.

Some people think our spelling
should be simplified. What does the
group think of this idea? What
problems do they forsee? **AT1/5d**

6 A *World Language* **AT1/5a-c**
Does the group think a world language
would help greater international
understanding?

7 *Changes in Language* **AT1/5a-c**
Ask the children to comment on how
their own language has changed as
they have grown older. Young children
are often taught a different
language:—
    pussy cat = cat, moo moo = cow,
    papap = car, baa lamb = lamb,
    chuff-chuff = train, etc.
Why are these words used? How many
more words can the children add to the
list?

8 *Accents* **AT1/5e**
Add to the collection of Cockney
rhyming slang. Do the children have
any local dialect phrases? Make a
collection of them.

9 *Written and Spoken English* **AT1/5e;
AT3/5c & e**
Look at the differences between
written Standard English and local
spoken dialects. Why are there these
differences? How did they come
about?

10 *What Did He Say?* **AT3/5c & e**
After experimenting with ways of
writing dialects and accents the
children could make puzzles and fun
displays trying to "translate" regional
accents into Standard English:—

e.g. *Tintintin* = It isn't in the tin.
(Yorkshire)
Eesedeedintdoitburraberreedid
= He said he didn't do it, but I bet
he did!
Mimamsezamgonnagerrong = My
mum says I'm going to get wrong
(i.e. get into trouble).

11 *Dialect Poems* **AT2/5a & b; AT3/5c & e**
Read a selection of dialect poems.
Translate some of them into Standard
English. Which version is preferred?
Why?
I Like That Stuff — Poems from many
cultures selected by Morag Styles
(Cambridge) has a number of dialect
poems, mainly West Indian. It also
contains a useful glossary of such
dialect words.

Follow-up activities:
1 *A Bypass* **Science AT5/5c**
Is there a bypass near your school? Find
out when and why it was built. How did
the local people feel about its
construction at the time? Have they
changed their views now? Can they say
why?
Try to find photographs before,
during and after the building of the
bypass. Try your local library or
newspaper for news cuttings about it.
What differences are there between a
bypass and a motorway? **AT2/5d**

2 *Traffic Survey* **Maths AT12/5a-c**
Are there busy roads near your school?
How can you find out how busy they are,
and what kind of traffic goes on them?
At what times is the road most busy? Is
this true for every day of the week? Give
reasons for your answers.
In what ways is the traffic controlled
on main roads? (traffic lights, pedestrian
crossings, yellow lines, white lines,
traffic signs etc.) How easy is it for
pedestrians to cross the road?
Can you think of ways to improve the
flow of traffic and/or make it easier for
pedestrians? **Technology AT2/5c**

3 *Traffic Congestion* **Science AT5/5c**
What ways can the group think of to
cope with congested streets without
building a bypass?

4 *Wild Flowers* **Science AT2/5a & d**
Why is it important to protect wild
flowers? The theme of conservation will
be explored more fully in Unit 6: 'A
Better World?'

5 *Re-telling Traditional Tales*   **AT1/5a & b**
   a) Re-tell well-known tales with the main character as story teller.
   b) Bring the stories up-to-date by setting them in modern times with different characters, but keeping to the same basic plot.   **AT2/5a & b**

6 *'Fairy Tales'*
   The computer program 'Fairy Tales' as mentioned in the pupil's book is available from Resource, Exeter Road, off Coventry Grove, Doncaster, DN2 4PY.

Name _____

Cars

In 1930 there were already 1 million cars in Britain. By 1940 the figure had increased to 1½ million. 2½ million cars were on the roads in 1950, and by 1960 the number had jumped to 5½ million. By 1970 the number of cars had doubled. In 1980 there were 16 million cars on Britain's roads.

Make a graph to show how the number of cars has increased on Britain's roads since 1930. If you can find more recent figures then include these too.

Graph to show _____

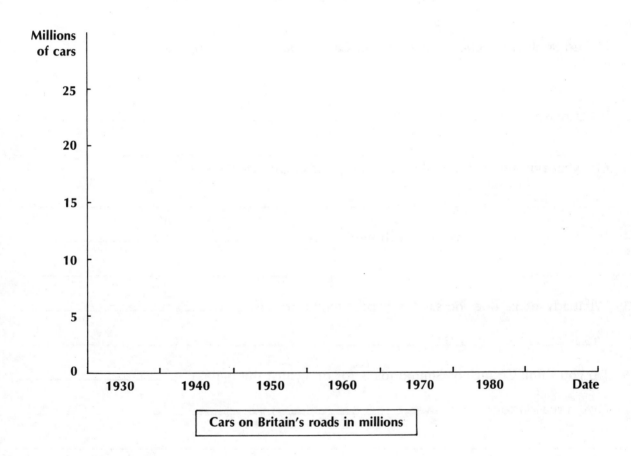

Cars on Britain's roads in millions

To think and write about
Answer these questions on the back of the sheet.

A

1 What do you notice about the rate of increase in the number of cars?

2 Can you think of an explanation for this?

3 Is it possible to forecast a figure for the next decade?

B

1 Make a list of the problems motorised transport has brought.

2 What would our world be like without motorised transport?

5.5a Modelling
© 1990 Collins Educational
AT3/5a

Name————————————

ENGLISH
ALIVE

Level 5
Master

5.5b

The Chadwick Bypass

1 Is Fred Sedley, the chef of the Carlton Café, in favour of the bypass?

——

2 What reason does he give for this? ——————————————————————

——

3 On what point does Councillor Joe Simmonds agree with Fred?

——

4 In what way does he disagree with him? ————————————————————

——

5 What advantage does he say the bypass might bring? ————————————

——

6 Do you think Councillor Simmonds is for or against the bypass? ——————

   Give a reason for your answer. —————————————————————————

——

——

7 What does he hope the result of the inquiry will be? ————————————

——

8 Both men refer to the traffic through Chadwick in ways which show how they feel about it.
   Listen to the cassette again.
   a) Which words does Fred use to show how important he thinks the traffic is

   to Chadwick? ——————————————————————————————————

   b) Which words tell us Councillor Simmonds' attitude to heavy lorries?

——

5.5b Listening skills
© 1990 Collins Educational
AT2/5b-c

Famous People

Use an encyclopedia to find out the important changes each person brought about.

1 William Wilberforce _____

_____

2 Lord Shaftesbury _____

_____

3 Elizabeth Fry _____

_____

4 James Brindley _____

_____

5 Florence Nightingale _____

_____

6 Lord Beveridge _____

_____

7 Emmeline Pankhurst _____

_____

8 Sir Frank Whittle _____

_____

5.5c Fact find
© 1990 Collins Educational
AT2/5d

Fact Find: Language

Use the *Guinness Book of Records* to find the answers to these questions.

1 How many words are there in the English language? _____

2 How many of these does the average person use:

   a) in speech? _____

   b) in writing? _____

3 What is the longest word in the Oxford English Dictionary? _____

4 What are the longest palindromes in the English language? _____

_____

5 What is the shortest holo-alphabetic sentence? _____

_____

6 What do you think an holo-alphabetic sentence is? _____

_____

7 Make up your own holo-alphabetic sentence. _____

_____

_____

8 What are the shortest place names in

   a) the world? _____

   b) Great Britain? _____

9 What is the longest place name in

   a) Great Britain? _____

   b) England? _____

   c) Scotland? _____

   d) Ireland? _____

10 Which word has the most homophones? _____
Choose five of its meanings and write a sentence for each one on the back of this sheet.

Name _____

Americanisms

Complete the chart by matching the English words with their American counterparts.

elevator	sidewalk	sweets	line	underpass
drawing pin	apartment	druggist	petrol	railway
subway	truck	caretaker	molasses	paraffin
cupboard	tin	holiday		

English	American
chemist	_____
_____	candy
treacle	_____
_____	closet
_____	kerosene
flat	_____
_____	thumb tack
_____	gas (oline)
pavement	_____
underground railway	_____
subway	_____
_____	railroad
lorry	_____
_____	janitor
_____	vacation
lift	_____
queue	_____
_____	can

Do you know any more Americanisms? If so, make your own list.

5.5e Americanisms
© 1990 Collins Educational
ATS1-4

... each prefix. Think about their meanings and try to guess the meaning

... your guess.

Add one ... ach list.

mono-
monotonous
monorail
monocle
monopoly

_____

I think **mono-** means _____

_____

bi-
bicycle
bifocal
biplane
binocular

_____

I think **bi-** means _____

_____

tri-
tripod
triangle
tricycle

_____

I think **tri-** means _____

_____

auto-
autograph
autobiography
automatic

_____

I think **auto-** means _____

_____

bio-
biology
biography
biochemistry

_____

I think **bio-** means _____

_____

pre-
prehistoric
precaution
prepare
prefix

_____

I think **pre-** means _____

_____

Name _____

ENGLISH
ALIVE

Level 5
Master

5.5g

The Future Tense

The future tense of a verb is made by putting *shall* or *will* before the main verb.

We use *shall* with *I* and *we*.   We use *will* with *you, he, she, it* and *they*.

| I shall try.   You will try.   We shall go.   They will go. |

A   Complete this chart.

Present	Future
I speak	I shall speak
we hurry	_____
he sends	_____
she saves	_____
they fly	_____
we take	_____
it lands	_____
he laughs	_____
we go	_____
they draw	_____
I read	_____
it sticks	_____

B   Put the future tense of the verb in brackets in the space.

1   I _____ at the concert tonight. (sing)

2   They _____ a meal for us. (cook)

3   We _____ the area tomorrow. (explore)

4   He _____ us with all the necessary materials. (supply)

5   I _____ the outside of the house. (paint)

6   It _____ very sunny. (is)

Justice: Part 1

Sandra looked through her bedroom window at a glorious summer day.

'It just isn't fair!' she shouted. She ran downstairs to her mother.

'Mum, please let me go out. It's the best day we've had in weeks. It's not fair to keep me in.'

'Now listen to me, Sandra,' said Mrs. Lewis. 'You know why you are being kept in. Mrs. Williams' window was broken yesterday, and she said you did it. You and that silly gang of yours.'

'But I didn't break it! We weren't anywhere near Mrs. Williams'. We were. . .' Her voice died away. She couldn't really tell her mum where the Treetop Gang had been playing. She wasn't supposed to go near the reservoir.

'You were seen, Sandra,' pointed out her mother.

'Fiona Walker never saw me! She couldn't have. She's just trying to get her own back on our gang because we wouldn't let her join.'

She looked out of the window in frustration. 'Anyway, I'm paying my share of the repair bill, aren't I? Would you change your mind if I did some housework for you?'

'Thank you, but I'm not making any promises,' her mother replied.

To think and talk about

1   What sort of girl do you think Sandra is?

2   Do you think her mother is being fair with her?
    How would you feel if you were Sandra?

3   Do you think her mother will let her out?
    Can you give a reason for your answer?

5.5h Group prediction — 1
© 1990 Collins Educational
AT1/5b; AT2/5b

Justice: Part 2

'Well, she's obviously not coming, said Lewie, the leader of the Treetop Gang. 'She's probably been kept in by her mother. We'll go without her.'

'You're sure this is the right thing to do, Lewie?' asked a voice.

'You're a real wet you are, Jamie Crowther,' came the reply. 'I've explained it all to you. We didn't break Williams' window, so it's not right to expect the gang to chip in and pay for it.' The gang shouted their agreement. 'But if we've been blamed for breaking a window, and charged for it too, then it's only right that we should have the satisfaction of smashing one.'

'Yes!' cried the gang.

'Justice is on our side,' continued their leader, 'but don't let's get seen doing it, right? Grown-ups don't always see things the way they really are.'

'Who's going to throw the stone?' asked Denny Harris.

'Me,' announced Lewie, 'and it's going to be a great big one. Let's go!'

To think and talk about

1   What do you think of Lewie's opinions? Do you agree with any of them? Which don't you agree with? Can you say why?

2   What sort of a person would you say Lewie is?

3   How many different ways do you think the story might develop? Which is your group's most sensible suggestion? Can you say why? Which is the least sensible suggestion? What makes you think so?

5.5i Group prediction — 2
© 1990 Collins Educational
AT1/5b; AT2/5b

Name_____

ENGLISH
ALIVE

Level 5
Master

5.5j

Justice: Part 3

'About the parish jumble sale,' began the Rev. Michael Newman. He was sitting in Mrs. Williams' new sun lounge with views all the way across to Sunbury Woods, 'and on a clear day to the Isle of Wight,' as she had told him twice already. He took another sip from his teacup and went on. 'I think the best date would be. . .'

At that moment a large stone came crashing through one of the panes, missing Mrs. Williams by inches. The Rev. Newman's teacup slid off his knee and smashed on the 'imported Italian floor tiles'.

'Goodness me!' cried the clergyman, beginning to quiver with shock. Mrs. Williams had more presence of mind. She leapt out of her chair, crunched her way through broken glass and hurried through the sliding glass door. A face was looking over the hedge, but disappeared as the Rev. Newman came on to the patio.

'It's that Sandra again!' screamed Mrs. Williams in fury.

'I'm not so sure about that,' said the still-shaking Rev. Newman.

'Of course it was her!' she insisted. 'I'm going straight down to her mother this instant. The cheek of the girl!'

To think and talk about

1   Is this what you expected would happen? Why?

2   From what you know about Mrs. Williams and Sandra's mother what do you think will happen when she arrives with her complaint?

3   How do you think the story will end?

4   Imagine you are the author. Which of the group's suggestions would make the most interesting ending? Can you say why?

5.5j   Group prediction — 3
© 1990 Collins Educational
AT1/5b; AT2/5b

Justice: Part 4

Mrs. Williams rang the doorbell long and hard.

'Dear me, Mrs. Williams,' said Sandra's mother, 'whatever is the matter?'

'Your Sandra has smashed another of my windows!'

Mrs. Lewis was quite taken aback.

'You'd better come in,' she said. She showed her irate guest to a chair and waited for her to calm down.

'Are you quite sure about all this?' she asked when Mrs. Williams had told her the story.

'Quite sure, and the Rev. Michael Newman is my witness.'

Sandra's mother began to regret allowing her daughter out.

'It's partly my fault,' she said, 'I let her go out because it was such a beautiful day.' At that moment she spotted her daughter coming up the drive.

'Here she is. Let's see what she has to say for herself.' They sat in silence, as the front door opened and closed. Lewie Lewis, the leader of the Treetop Gang came into the room.

'Sandra Lewis,' began her mother, 'come here and explain yourself!'

To think and talk about

1   Did the ending surprise you? Can you say why? Look back over the story and see how the author hid the fact that Sandra and Lewie were the same person. What clues are there that might have helped you?

2   Have your ideas about Sandra changed since Part 1? Can you say why? How do you think she feels now?

3   Has justice really been done? Say why you think so.

5.5k   Group prediction — 4
© 1990 Collins Educational
AT1/5b; AT2/5b

A Conversation

Think about these questions, and then discuss them with your group.

1 Why did John assume Chris Taylor was a man?
   Did you assume this too? Why was that?

2 a) What is a 'sexist' remark?
   b) What do you think Stephanie means by a 'male chauvinist pig'?

3 Do you think John's criticism of women drivers is fair? Why?

4 What do you think of Stephanie's criticism of men drivers?

5 What do you think of John's explanation of why women drivers have fewer accidents?

6 Why do you think John says advanced motoring is 'a good thing for a woman to do'?

7 Discuss how John shows his attitude:
   a) to women in general;
   b) to Stephanie;
   c) to his wife.

8 Discuss Stephanie's view of John.

9 Do you agree with anything said by John or Stephanie? Give reasons for your answer.

10 Which points do you disagree with? Give your own point of view.

5.51 Listening skills
© 1990 Collins Educational
AT1/5b; AT2/5b

Unit 6

Theme — A Better World?
Stimuli — from 'Alpha-B75-Earth Visitors'
      Guide' by John Cunliffe,
      included in *Spaceways*
      compiled by John Foster, OUP
      'Fish in a Polluted River' by Ian
      Serraillier, from *I'll Tell You a
      Tale*, Longman
      from *The Calf of the November
      Cloud* — Hilary Ruben, Collins
      'The Song of the Whale' by Kit
      Wright, from *Hot Dog & Other
      Poems*, Kestrel
      from *A Rag, a Bone and a Hank of
      Hair* — Nicholas Fisk, Kestrel
      'The Horses' by Edwin Muir, Faber
      and Faber Ltd.
      'The Cry' by Edvard Munch, Oslo
      Municipal Art Gallery
      From *On The Run* by Nina
      Bawden, Victor Gollancz &
      Puffin

AT1 Speaking/listening
5b explaining how and why things happen
5b dealing with problems in the imagination
5b speculation
5b taking part in discussion
5c planning a speech
5d group presentation: TV points of view programme

AT2 Reading
5a expressing preferences
5b inference
5b speculation
5b sorting sentences by subject and sequencing them
5b imaginative response
5b evaluation
5b picture: Munch — "The Cry"
5b cloze procedure
5b, d reading for details
5d using a dictionary
5d modelling: flow chart
5d labelled diagram: explaining what is happening
5d using reference books
5e author's choice of words

AT3 Writing
Poetic:
5a-b, d, e essay
5a-b, d, e "tree" poems
5a-b, d, e poem about an endangered species
5a-e completing a story
Transactional:
5a keeping record charts
5a designing a poster
5a-b, e replying to an invitation
5a, d making notes
5a-e design a game: "Save Our Planet"
5a-e imaginative response to a painting: "The Cry"
5a-e description of what life might be like in a hundred years' time
5d planning "Planet Earth" TV programme

Cloze passage:
The actual words used by the author in this extract are given here for reference purposes only. They should not be regarded as the "correct" answers.
1) walked 2) parks 3) animal 4) way
5) like 6) clean 7) touch 8) the
9) mewed 10) following 11) line 12) one
13) look 14) would 15) him 16) it
17) and 18) the 19) and 20) computer
21) Brin 22) Parks 23) shrubs 24) A
25) him 26) of

Activity sheets:
5.6a recycling paper: following instructions **AT2/5d**
5.6b making papier mâché: modelling — picture strip **AT2/5d; AT3/5a**
5.6c listening skills: detecting emotionally charged words/persuasion and pressure **AT1/5b; AT2/5b; AT2/5d; AT3/5a-e**
5.6d group prediction: *Aliens* — 1 **AT1/5b; AT2/5b**
5.6e group prediction: *Aliens* — 2 **AT1/5b; AT2/5b**
5.6f group prediction: *Aliens* — 3 **AT1/5b; AT2/5b**
5.6g group prediction: *Aliens* — 4 **AT1/5b; AT2/5b**
5.6h Assessment Master: writing skills **AT3/5a-e**
5.6i Assessment Master: reading skills — 1 **AT2/5b**
5.6j Assessment Master: reading skills — 2 **AT2/5b & d**
5.6k Assessment Master: assignment — Adventure Island **AT1/5d; AT3/5a & d**

Listening skills: AT1/5b; AT2/5b & d; AT3/5a-e

5.6c detecting emotionally charged words/persuasion and pressure

Side 2, track 5. Tape counter _____

Samantha tries to persuade her fiancé, Charles, to buy her a fur from a department store. As she tries on a mink stole her friend Angela dissuades her from the purchase by a combination of persuasion and pressure.

As the questions are designed to stimulate discussion, there is no answer card for this sheet.

Assessment Masters

Assessment Masters **5.6h-5.6j** are designed as test papers. They may be used as a formal test and as such marked to give a percentage.

Assessment Master **5.6k** is named *Adventure Island.* It is intended as a group assignment involving the planning of a leisure park on an island, taking into account a number of factors. It gives opportunity for discussion and problem solving and the presentation of the findings in the form of a plan and promotion brochure.

5.6h *Writing* **AT3/5a-e**

completing sentences (8 marks per sentence)	8
direct speech (an allowance of 12 marks)	12
EITHER narrative prose	
OR a newspaper article	30
	50

5.6i *Reading — 1* **AT2/5b**

prose passage comprehension	
Nos.1-7: 2 marks each	14
No. 8: 6 marks	6
	20

5.6j *Reading — 2* **AT2/5b & d**

Reading a diagram of a bottle garden and writing instructions on how to make one	10
Modelling: cycle diagram	10
Cloze passage (adjectives)	10
	30
	TOTAL = 100%

Skills breakdown:

Writing skills	50%
Reading skills	50%
	100%

Cloze passage:

The adjectives deleted from the passage on 5.6j are given here. Any other words which fit the context are perfectly acceptable.
1) musty 2) dim 3) old 4) long 5) dark 6) thick 7) enormous 8) red 9) pitted 10) soft

Whether used informally or not the Assessment Masters can establish where weaknesses lie and further practice is needed.

Suggestions for further practice:
Writing:
story, Book 4: 16, 51, **4.3N**; Book 5: 11, 83
plot, Book 4 p. 28
description, Book 4 pp. 3 & 50; Book 5: 21, 28-9, 48, 70, 93
giving instructions, Book 4 pp. 10, 21, 53; Book 5: 93
punctuation, Book 4: pp. 8-9, **4.3f**
direct speech, Book 4: 8-9, 17-18, **4.1e**, **4.93**; Book 5: 2, 40-1, 80, **5.3g**, **5.3h**, **5.3N**
checking spelling, Book 5 p. 77

Reading:
main idea, Book 4: 22-3, 36-7, 41, 48, 67, **4.4N**; Book 5: 36, 62, **5.3k-5.3n**
reorganising information: lists, Book 5 p. 62
explaining a diagam, Book 5 p. 46, 89
cloze, Book 4: 3, 38, 49, **4.2d**, **4.4N**; Book 5: 49, **5.4b**, 94

Speaking/listening:

1 *Persuasion* **AT1/5a & b**
Split the group into pairs. Give each pair a situation in which one person attempts to persuade the other to do something, e.g. do some homework, run an errand, play a game, etc. etc.

2 *Refuse Disposal* **Science AT5/5b; AT13/5a & b**
What happens to the refuse in your district? How is it collected? What happens to it then? Is any of it incinerated? What further problems does incineration cause? Which items are salvaged? **AT1/5a-d; AT2/5d**
Find out where the bottle banks are in your area. What happens to the glass? Why are the colours separated? How is coloured glass made? Is there a scrapyard for cars? What happens to them there?

3 *Rag and Bone Men* **Science AT5/5b; AT13/5a & b**
Are there any rag and bone men in your district? Find out about them? What do

they collect? What do they do with the junk they collect? **AT1/5a & b**

4 *Pollution* **AT2/5d; AT1/5a & b**
What is being done to reduce pollution in your district?

5 *Problems of Town Life* **AT3/5a**
Make a list of the problems of living in modern towns and cities, e.g. overcrowding, high-rise flats, traffic dangers, pollution, vandalism and noise. What can be done to solve these problems? Find out the problems of life in towns in earlier times, e.g. sanitation, slums, etc. How many of these problems have disappeared? Which are still with us? How many have got worse? Are there any lessons to be learned here? **Science AT14/5c**

Design a town of the future to solve as many of these problems as possible. **Technology AT1-5**

6 *Future Energy Sources* **AT1/5a & b**
Discuss future sources of energy such as power from the sun, from the wind and from the sea. **Science AT13/5a & b**

7 *Conservation* **Science AT2**
Study trees and plants and the insect life which is found on them. An oak tree supports the widest range of wild life. Make a list of the creatures it supports.

Practical conservation work might include making a bird table or planting trees. **AT1/5a-d**

8 *Waste Land* **Technology AT1-5**
Is there a plot of waste land nearby? Are there any plans for its use? If not plan how it might be used. Consider leisure needs. Can any part of it be used as a conservation area for wild life? Is any part of the site of any historical value, such as old buildings? Can anything be done to preserve some of this history? **Science AT5/5c**

Map and sketch the area. Take photographs. Discuss with your group how the site might best be developed. Make new plans and sketches to match your ideas. **AT1/5a-d**

Evaluate your conclusions. Are they feasible? Would money be available for the development? How would you protect the developed plot from vandalism?

9 *Drought and Famine* **AT2/5d**
Has the group ever been really hungry? How is famine different from this? What is the difference between drought and famine? How does the one lead to the other?

What causes drought? Use an atlas or globe to locate the countries where drought is a problem. Which of these countries are rich and which are poor? Do the rich countries also suffer from famine? Why not? What do they do about it? What happens in poor countries? What can be done to help them?

Discuss other natural disasters such as hurricanes, earthquakes and floods.

10 *Wars* **AT1/5a-d**
It is a sad fact of modern life that, sitting in the comfort and safety of our homes, we can witness the brutality of war on our television screens. Discuss the effect this has.

Discuss why wars happen. Who suffers during a war: soldiers? politicians? ordinary people? How can wars be prevented?

11 *Animal Rights* **AT1/5a-d; AT2/5d**
Follow up side 2, track 5 of the listening skills tape and sheet **5.6c** with a discussion of animal rights. What rights should animals have?

Examine such issues as the killing of animals for food and fur, and the use of animals to test drugs and cosmetics.

12 *Endangered Animals* **AT1/5a-d; AT2/5d**
Make a list of animals which have become extinct over the last few centuries. How many of these have disappeared over the last hundred years? Why have they become extinct? Which animals are currently endangered? What can be done to preserve them? Why is it necessary to do so? Why is it just as important to preserve the habitats of these creatures?

13 *Leaving Earth* **AT1/5a-d**
Suppose you were leaving Earth to start a new life on another planet: what would you take with you? Give reasons for your answers.

Follow up work:

1 *Rubbish at School* **Science AT5/5b**
Find how much rubbish is thrown away at your school every week. Classify it into types of rubbish.

Use junk materials for creative work.

2 *Compost* **Science AT7/5b**
Make a compost heap. Find out what happens as plant waste changes into rich compost.

3 *Clean-up Campaign* **Science AT2/5c**
Tidy up the area round the school. Wear plastic gloves when handling litter. Enlist the help of the local council to remove larger items.

4 *Collecting for Charity* **Science AT5/5b**
Many charities make use of our unwanted items. Boy scouts often have collections of unwanted newspapers, milk bottle tops and ring pulls from canned drinks. Find out if any local charities are collecting such items and send along any you can find.

5 *Make a Ring-pull Chain*
Collect ring pulls and make them into a chain. How long is your chain after a week? a month? a year?

6 *Air Pollution Experiments* **Science AT13/5a & b; AT7/5c; AT5/5a**

a) Sulphur Dioxide
When fossil fuels are burnt they give off sulphur dioxide in the smoke. Even the tall chimneys of factories and power stations cannot stop this gas finding its way back to earth.

This simple experiment shows the effect of sulphur dioxide gas on plants.

1 Put a pot of cress into a plastic bag.
2 Crush a campden tablet, add two teaspoonsfuls of lemon juice (to produce sulphur dioxide), and add to the plastic bag.
3 Put a second tub of cress into a plastic bag as a control experiment.
4 Examine both tubs after two days. Record the results.

b) Dirt in Rain **Science AT5/5a; AT9/5c**
Another way of testing for air pollution is to see how much dirt the rain brings down with it.

1 Fold a filter paper into a cone and fit it into the neck of a milk bottle.
2 Put the bottle outside when it is raining and after a few hours bring it indoors and lay the filter paper out on a saucer.
3 Wet a second piece of filter paper with tap water and lay that on another saucer.
4 Add a few drops of plant food to 500ml of cooled boiled water.

(Boiling the water will kill off any spores that may be present.)
5 Keep both filter papers moist with the plant food solution.
6 Cover the plates with transparent bowls and leave them in a light place for several days, observing them regularly.
7 After a few days you may find green patches on the filter paper — these are single-celled plants called algae. If moss spores grow you will see fine green threads on the paper. Fungi produce white, grey or blue patches.
8 Compare the growth on the two filter papers. What conclusions do you reach?

7 *Water Pollution Experiments* **Science AT5/5a; AT2/5c**
Dirty or polluted water in rivers and streams is sometimes called 'turbid'. Because of the dirt, turbid water cuts out sunlight and as a result plants cannot grow.

You can test water samples to find their turbidity levels.

Collect water samples from rainwater, puddle water, local streams, etc.

To make a turbidity tester cut a strip of tape the length of a clear plastic bottle. Mark the tape in cm and mm and stick it into the bottle. Drop a coin into the bottle. Slowly pour one type of water into your tester. Stop pouring when it becomes difficult to read the lettering on the coin. (Read the coin by looking down through the top of the bottle.) Record the depth of water. Pour it back into its original bottle and try the next sample. Compare the results.

8 *Pioneer 10* **AT2/5d**
In 1972 the space probe Pioneer 10 was launched. It has since sent back pictures and information about the planets of the Solar System. The probe carries a special plaque to explain its origin to an alien life form.

The man and woman pictured are standing in front of the probe to indicate their size.

The radiating lines represent the positions of pulsars, which are sources of cosmic radio energy. They are arranged to show our sun as the centre

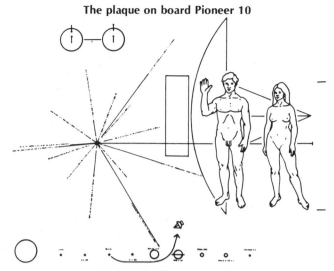

The plaque on board Pioneer 10

of our civilisation.

The diagram of the planets at the bottom of the plaque shows where the probe was launched from and its route out of the solar system. At the top is a diagram of the hydrogen atom. Hydrogen can be used to help an alien civilisation work out when the probe was launched.

Can the group work out what information the plaque contains? Why are there no words? Can the children devise a similar message about themselves?

9 *Time Capsule* **AT1/5a-d**
In Level 2 we suggested burying a time capsule in the school grounds. If this has not already been dug up, why not do so now?

Take time examining the contents of the capsule. What has changed over the intervening years. How have the ideas and tastes of the children changed?

Add new material and re-bury the capsule for a future generation. They will be most interested to read of your hopes and fears for the future of our planet.

10 *Information Technology*
Technology AT5
We have already introduced children to information technology by using the computer, word processing and data bases. Further uses of IT include teletext, Prestel, spelling checkers, desk-top publishing software and a computer/telephone link-up called a modem. Modems allow messages to be sent from the computer keyboard to other computers. Databases such as Telecom Gold may be accessed from the school computer although most organisations make charges to which the cost of the call needs to be added. Many schools are, however, willing to pay this cost as it demonstrates the power of modern technology to receive and process information.

11 *Some Recommended Poems*
AT2/5a & b
'The Newcomer' by Brian Patten, in *A Fourth Poetry Book,* Oxford
'A Souvenir' by John Kitching, in *A Second Poetry Book,* Oxford
'The Ark' by Stanley Cook
'Towards the Stars' by Iain Crichton Smith
  both in *Spaceways,* compiled by John Foster, Oxford
'The Earthling' by Brian Patten, in *Gangsters, Ghosts and Dragonflies*

Useful Addresses:
Information on animal protection and conservation may be obtained from the organisations below. Please remember to enclose a stamped addressed envelope if you write to them.
Fauna and Flora Preservation Society
8-12 Camden High Street, London NW1 0JH
Has information about ponds, bat boxes and various campaigns.
Royal Society for the Prevention of Cruelty to Animals
RSPCA Headquarters, Causeway, Horsham, West Sussex RH12 1HG
Offers advice on keeping pets, and information about cruelty to animals.
Royal Society for the Protection of Birds
The Young Ornithologists' Club:
The Lodge, Sandy, Beds SG19 2DL
The club has a magazine six times a year with information, quizzes and competitions.
Watch Club/Royal Society for Nature Conservation
The Green, Nettleham, Lincoln LN12 2NR
For information about conservation and nature projects.
World Wide Fund for Nature
Panda House, Weyside Park, Godalming, Surrey GU7 1XR
For information about wild animals in danger throughout the world.

Young People's Trust for Endangered Species
19 Quarry St., Guildford, Surrey GU1 3EH
This is a world-wide campaign to save
endangered species and wild places. The
trust organises special junior field study
courses for the age range 9-13. They have
raised money to fund the scientific study of
whales.

Name———————————————

ENGLISH
ALIVE

Level 5
Master

5.6a

Instructions for Recycling Paper

Any paper will do for recycling, but newspaper is by far the most common and most manageable form of discarded paper.

1   Tear up the newspaper into small pieces and put them into a bucket.

2   Cover the paper with boiling water. Beat it to a pulp with a stick. Leave to cool.

3   Use an old liquidiser to liquidise the pulp, one handful at a time. Add plenty of water and liquidise until smooth.

4   Put pulp in a deep bowl and add more water until the mixture is very sloppy.

5   Make a deckle and mould from two wooden rectangular frames, one of which should be covered with a medium mesh.

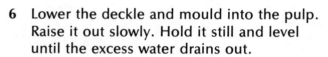

6   Lower the deckle and mould into the pulp. Raise it out slowly. Hold it still and level until the excess water drains out.

7   Remove the deckle and carefully turn the mould on to a "couching cloth" (felt or other absorbent material).

8   Mop up any excess water and gently rub the mesh of the mould with a cloth to release the pulp.

9   Remove the mould leaving the "paper" on the couching cloth. Cover with another couching cloth.

10   Iron the cloth until the paper between is nearly dry.

11   Carefully peel the paper from between the layers of cloth.

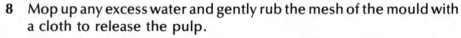

12   Hang up to dry, or dry flat for a smoother result.

13   Your recycled paper is now ready to be re-used.

Alternatives
Because re-cycled paper is a dirty grey colour, it looks dingy and dull. Experiment by adding coloured inks to the pulp before moulding.

5.6a Re-cycling paper
© 1990 Collins Educational
AT2/5d

Name————————————

Making Papier Mâché

Look at these instructions for how to use old paper to make papier mâché models. Study the instructions carefully, and then on a separate sheet draw a series of captioned pictures showing how to do it.

1 Tear the paper into small, manageable pieces.

2 Use lolly sticks, matches or pipe cleaners to form the skeleton of the model you intend to make.

3 Attach your skeleton to a board with plasticine or tape to keep it firm.

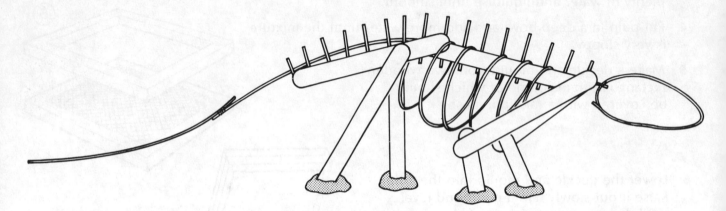

4 Cover the skeleton with a layer of damp paper pieces.

5 Cover the damp paper with a layer of paste, e.g. wallpaper paste.

6 Add a layer of paper.

7 Repeat steps 5 and 6, six more times, leaving each layer to dry before adding the next one.

8 Paint and varnish your model.

Make models of some of the world's most endangered species as part of your group work on pollution and conservation.

Blue whale

African elephant

5.6b Making papier mache
© 1990 Collins Educational
AT2/5d; AT3/5a

The Mink Stole

Think about these questions and then discuss them with your group.

Persuasion

1 How does Samantha persuade Charles to consider buying her a mink stole?

2 How does the shop assistant interest Samantha in a real fur?

3 What arguments does Angela use to dissuade Samantha from buying a real fur?

4 What words does she use to shock Samantha?

5 What is said which finally persuades Samantha not to buy a real fur?

6 Why is this such a forceful argument?

7 How does the shop assistant interest Samantha in an artificial fur?

Points of View

1 Do you agree with Angela's views? Give reasons for your answer.

2 What do you think of Samantha's counter-arguments?

3 What do you think Charles feels about the outcome of the situation?

Something to do

1 Find out which animals are killed for their fur.

2 Explain in writing your views on the subject.

5.6c Listening skills
© 1990 Collins Educational
AT1/5b; AT2/5b; AT2/5d; AT3/5a-e

Name _____

Aliens: Part 1

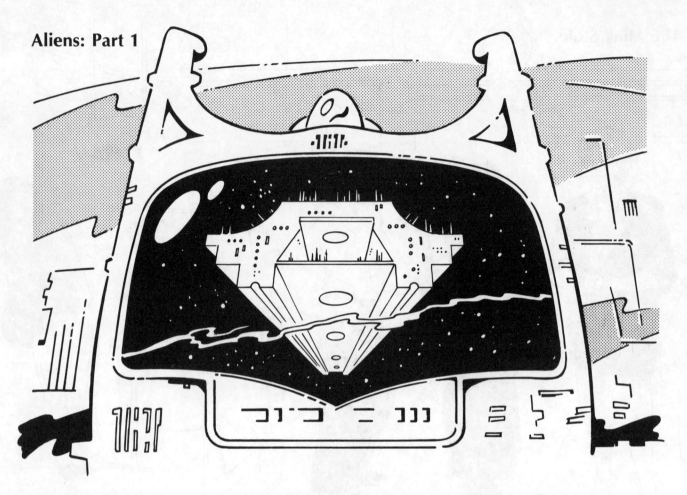

The alien ship was just detectable by the long range scanner. Commander Shan ordered an intercept course and the Federation survey craft moved into hyper-drive.

'Intercept in twelve minutes,' announced Su, the ship's computer.

'Bio-scanner range in two minutes.'

The bio-scanners began to register life on the alien craft, but the readings bore no comparison to any life-readings in the computer data banks. After a pause Su made another announcement.

'The occupants have body temperatures just sufficient to support basic life functions.'

'Speculate,' said Commander Shan.

'My primary function is to seek and provide information,' said Su.

'Your secondary function is to process that information and arrive at conclusions,' pointed out the Commander. 'Speculate!'

'Speculation: the occupants of the craft are in cryogenic suspension.'

'Explain.'

'Cryogenic suspension is an ancient method of prolonging life by freezing the body at extremely low temperatures. It was used in space flight as a solution to the problems of inter-galactic transport. Before the invention of hyper-drive such voyages took thousands of years. Crew members were put into cryogenic suspension at the beginning of each voyage, and re-animated at its end. Their bodies aged only a few days during the entire voyage.' Su paused. 'The craft is now in Close-scan range.'

The control screen was filled with a three-dimensional image of the alien ship. It was vast, bigger than any Federation ship. There were strange signs and symbols on its side.

'Jo, Kris,' said Commander Shan to a second screen, 'Prepare to tele-port.'

To think and talk about

What do you think Jo and Kris will find? What dangers might they face?

Aliens: Part 2

Jo and Kris materialised in the central control room of the alien craft. As Kris reported their arrival on his communicator, Jo did a bio-search of the room. It was without life, and almost without light too. There was the faintest hum from the control banks, and just the occasional glimmer of a dial. Jo touched a button on her suit and light spread around her from some invisible source. She increased the range of the bio-sensor and detected life outside the room. To her relief the light remained blue, indicating no threat.

They left the control room through a sliding door and found themselves in a corridor. As they proceeded along it the bio-sensor readings grew stronger. Another sliding door admitted them into a vast chamber completely filled with bank after bank of sealed capsules.

'The cryogenic suspension units,' observed Kris. He leaned forward to look through the transparent windows, but there was too much frosting to see the creatures clearly.

'Look!' gasped Jo. She was pointing to a label above the window. The symbols were completely indecipherable, but there was a clear three-dimensional picture. Kris was filled with revulsion for the horrible creature. They backed away in disgust, failing to notice that the bio-sensor was now flashing a warning.

To think and talk about

1 Would you say Commander Shan was wise in sending Jo and Kris aboard the alien ship? Say why you think so.

2 What danger do you think they are in now?

3 Talk about what might happen next. Which is the most likely suggestion? Why? Which is the least likely? Can you say why?

5.6e Group prediction — 2
© 1990 Collins Educational
AT1/5b; AT2/5b

Name _____

ENGLISH
ALIVE

Level 5
Master

5.6f

Aliens: Part 3

It was Jo who noticed the alien. It was standing at the end of the aisle, holding a weapon. The horror of its appearance delayed her for the few micro seconds it took the creature to leap out of sight. She began to run down the aisle firing repeatedly as she went. The chamber resonated with the soft explosions of her weapon. Kris followed her, his gun raised to cover her. When they reached the end of the aisle the alien was nowhere to be seen, but the bio-sensor pointed them down another corridor. Its warning light now flashed bright magenta.

The voice of Commander Shan came on the communicator.

'Jo? Kris? Report, please.' Jo gave him a short account of events. 'There are transmissions coming from the craft now,' Commander Shan told them. 'They're completely unintelligible, but there is a repetitive pattern. It's probably a distress call. You must silence it.'

The bio-sensor readings led them to the alien. They found it making strange noises into a metal stalk. It turned and raised a weapon at their approach, but this time Jo was prepared. The creature was caught in her destructor beam and vaporised.

To think and talk about

1 Do you think it was sensible to kill the alien? Had Jo any other choice?

2 Do you think they are now out of danger? Talk about how you think the story might end. Which idea would make the most interesting ending? Can you say why?

5.6f Group prediction — 3
© 1990 Collins Educational
AT1/5b; AT2/5b

Name

ENGLISH
ALIVE

Level 5
Master

5.6g

Aliens: Part 4

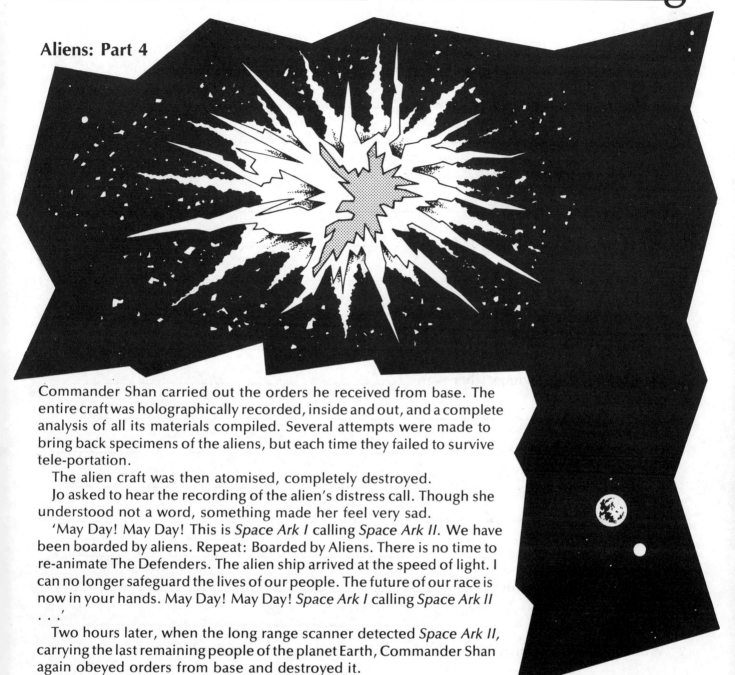

Commander Shan carried out the orders he received from base. The entire craft was holographically recorded, inside and out, and a complete analysis of all its materials compiled. Several attempts were made to bring back specimens of the aliens, but each time they failed to survive tele-portation.

The alien craft was then atomised, completely destroyed.

Jo asked to hear the recording of the alien's distress call. Though she understood not a word, something made her feel very sad.

'May Day! May Day! This is *Space Ark I* calling *Space Ark II*. We have been boarded by aliens. Repeat: Boarded by Aliens. There is no time to re-animate The Defenders. The alien ship arrived at the speed of light. I can no longer safeguard the lives of our people. The future of our race is now in your hands. May Day! May Day! *Space Ark I* calling *Space Ark II* . . .'

Two hours later, when the long range scanner detected *Space Ark II*, carrying the last remaining people of the planet Earth, Commander Shan again obeyed orders from base and destroyed it.

To think and talk about

1   Did the ending surprise you? How did it make you feel? If Commander Shan, Jo and Kris had been Earth people would you feel differently about the ending? Would this have made the destruction of the aliens right? Can you say why you think so?

2   Have your feelings about the main characters changed now you know they were aliens? Would you say they were cruel or destructive? Did you think so as you were reading the story? Can you say why?

3   Why do you think Jo was sad as she listened to the recording? Would you expect aliens to feel like this? Why?

4   Why do you think the Space Arks were destroyed? Had Commander Shan any other choice? What would you have done? Why?

5   Read the story again. How does the author make us feel sympathetic towards the *real* aliens? Do you think his only reason is to shock us at the end, or might he have some other purpose? If so, what do you think it is?

5.6g   Group prediction — 4
© 1990 Collins Educational
AT1/5b; AT2/5b

Name————————————

ENGLISH
ALIVE

Level 5
Master

5.6h

Writing

1 Complete these sentences in an interesting way.

a) The ring was stolen by a man who ————————————

———————————————————————————————

b) I was late because ————————————————————

———————————————————————————————

c) He was digging a hole when ———————————————

———————————————————————————————

d) You could become a first class athlete if ————————————

———————————————————————————————

e) She ran to the window whenever —————————————

———————————————————————————————

f) Janet carefully explained why —————————————

———————————————————————————————

g) He was always afraid of the dark after ————————————

———————————————————————————————

h) When midnight struck ————————————————

———————————————————————————————

2 Write an imaginary conversation overheard on a bus. Use direct speech.

———————————————————————————————

———————————————————————————————

———————————————————————————————

———————————————————————————————

———————————————————————————————

———————————————————————————————

3 Write *either* a story entitled 'A Most Unusual Day'
   or an article for your local paper explaining the advantages of living in your area. Suggest
   improvements which would make it even more attractive.

Name_____

ENGLISH
ALIVE

Level 5
Master

5.6k

Adventure Island

Your group is asked to plan a leisure park on Adventure Island. Look at the map of the island and the features already there. Discuss the changes you might make. Here are some ideas to consider:
— car parks, toilets, cafes, restaurants, snack bars
— a scenic road around the island, with picnic spots, view points, etc.
— gardens and footpaths
— sporting facilities, including water sports
— rides and attractions
How many other facilities can you think of?
  Discuss all the options with your group, and decide how you will develop Adventure Island. Add your ideas to the map.

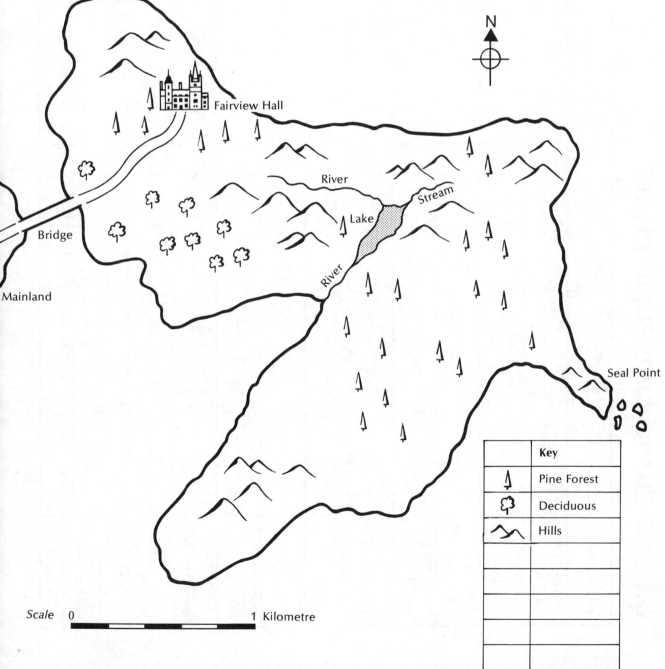

	Key
🌲	Pine Forest
🌳	Deciduous
⛰	Hills

Scale 0   1 Kilometre

5.6k Assessment Master
© 1990 Collins Educational
AT1/5d; AT3/5a & d

Design a brochure for Adventure Island showing everything it has to offer.

National Curriculum: Pupils profile

Level 5

English Alive Level 5	AT1 a	AT1 b	AT1 c	AT1 d	AT1 e	ATs1-4	AT2 a	AT2 b	AT2 c	AT2 d	AT2 e
Unit 1 Pupil's Book	5 10 15 11 12	4 7 12 17 10 11 15	4 10 15 16 11 12	13 17	13	9	12	3 12 7 17	14 15	6 8	7 12
Activity Sheets		a b c d				e f		a b j k c d i		14 h i	
Speaking/Listening	5 6 11 12 7 8 13 14	1 3 6 7 10 11 4 5 8 9 13 14	11 12	3 6 11						12	
Notes	7										
Follow-up Notes	4										
Unit 2 Pupil's Book		26 27				22 23		19 20 26 27 22 23 29 30	28 29 30	19 20 24 28 31 32 21 22 29 30 33	29
Activity Sheets						k		i m	m	a b e f c d g h	
Speaking/Listening	1 2 3 4	1 3	1 2 3	1 3							
Notes											
Follow-up Notes											
Unit 3 Pupil's Book	46 50	34 35 46 49 56 38 39 50 53	34 35 46 50	34 44 55 56 45 51			44 46	35 37 42 43 48 52 38 39 44 46 53 54	34 35 43 46 52 53 38 42 47 50 54	2 3 6 9 4 5	35 37 43 53 38 42 54
Activity Sheets		a b c d					q u	a b i j c d p u	i j p	f r s t	
Speaking/Listening	1 2 7 8 11 12 13 3 4 9 10 14 15 16	1 2 6 8 11 12 15 16 3 5 9 10 13 14	2 4 10	1 2 5 6 3 4 14 16					1 2 5 6 3 4 7		
Notes	7						8	8		2 12	
Follow-up Notes	14 15 17	14 15 16 17									
Unit 4 Pupil's Book								62 63 64 67	67	62 63 64 67	63
Activity Sheets	63	63	63	63	63	f		b		c d e g	
Speaking/Listening			63								
Notes											
Follow-up Notes							5	5			
Unit 5 Pupil's Book	83	71 72 83 73 80	83	71 72 73 83	83	74 75 77 81 e f g	82 83	68 69 73 74 79 82 71 72 75 76 83		69 71 75 76 73 74 77	79 82 83
Activity Sheets		h i j k						b h k i i j	b	c d	
Speaking/Listening	1 2 6 7 3 4	1 2 6 7 3 4	6 7	1 2 5	8 9						
Notes	5										
Follow-up Notes							11	11		9	
Unit 6 Pupil's Book		85 87 91 93 88 89 94	93	93			92 94	84 85 92 93 87 91 94		1 84 85 89 91 87 88 92 93	85 91 92
Activity Sheets		c d g e f		k				c d g i e f j		a b c j	
Speaking/Listening	1 2 6 7 11 12 3 4 8 10 13	1 2 6 7 11 12 3 4 8 10 13	2 7 11 12 8 10 13	2 7 11 12 8 10 13						2 4 11 12	
Notes											
Follow-up Notes	9						11	11		8	

English Alive Level 5	AT3 Writing a	b	c	d	e	AT4/5 Presentation a	b
Unit 1 Pupil's Book	3 4 9 10 17 / 5 8 13 16	3 5 13 16 / 9 10 17	3 5 13 16 / 9 10 17	3 4 10 16 / 9 13 17	3 5 13 16 / 9 10 17		3 4 10 16 / 5 9 13 17
Activity Sheets	g					f / e f / h	
Speaking/Listening Notes						5	
Follow-up Notes	1 2	1 2					
Unit 2 Pupil's Book	19 21 27 28 31 32 / 24 26 29 30 33	19 21 28 29 / 26 27 32 33	19 21 28 29 / 26 27 32 33	21 24 32 33 / 26 27 29	21 24 28 29 / 26 27 32 33	21 24 32 33 / 27 29	21 24 32 33 / 27 29
Activity Sheets	a ib / f						
Speaking/Listening Notes	1 2						
Follow-up Notes	3 5						
Unit 3 Pupil's Book	34 38 45 46 50 51 57 / 29 44 48 49 53 55	2 / 38 39 44 45 49 50 57 / 40 41 46 48 53 55	2 / 38 39 46 48 53 55 57 / 44 45 49 50 57	2 / 38 39 46 48 53 55 / 44 45 49 50 56	2 / 37 38 45 46 50 53 / 39 44 48 49 55 57	2 / 38 39 46 48 53 55 / 44 45 49 50 56	2 / 38 39 46 48 53 55 / 44 45 49 50 56
Activity Sheets	e g n o / h m p	u	u	u	u	u	u
Speaking/Listening Notes	1 2						
Follow-up Notes	8 10 13 / 11 12	8 10 13 / 11 12	12 13	12 13	9 12 / 13	12 13 / 12 13	12 13 / 12 13
Unit 4 Pupil's Book	64 67	64 67	64	64	64	64	64
Activity Sheets	a e / g	e / g	e / g	e / g		e / g	e / g
Speaking/Listening Notes							
Follow-up Notes							
Unit 5 Pupil's Book	71 72 82 83 / 73 78	71 72 80 81 / 73 78 82 83	71 72 / 73 82	71 72 82 83 / 73 78	71 72 83 / 73 82	74 75 71 72 82 83 / 77 80 73 78	71 72 82 83 / 73 78
Activity Sheets							
Speaking/Listening Notes	a						
Follow-up Notes						5	
Unit 6 Pupil's Book	85 87 91 92 95 / 88 89 93 94	85 89 93 94 / 91 92 95	91 93 / 94 95	87 89 93 94 / 91 92 95	85 89 93 94 / 91 92 95	87 89 93 94 / 91 92 95	87 89 93 94 / 91 92 95
Activity Sheets	b c / h k	c / h	c / h	c h / k	c / h	c h / k	c h / k
Speaking/Listening Notes	5	9 10 / 11	9 10 / 11	9 10 / 11	9 10 / 11		
Follow-up Notes	1						

Adventures in English Skills Chart with National Curriculum Attainment Targets and Levels

Book ▲
Program ●
Book and Program ○

AT1 Speaking & Listening

	Goblin Winter (Level 2)	Spooky Towers (Level 3)	Spellbound (Level 4)	Pirate's Treasure (Level 4)	Wreckers' Rock (Level 5)	McGinty's Gold (Level 5)	Common Confusions (Levels 3-5)	What is a Sentence? (Levels 3-5)
follow story and recall	●							
listen in discussion	●	●	●	●	●	●		
drama	▲	▲	▲	▲	▲	▲		
discuss constructively	●	●	●	●	●	●		

AT2 Reading

	Goblin Winter (Level 2)	Spooky Towers (Level 3)	Spellbound (Level 4)	Pirate's Treasure (Level 4)	Wreckers' Rock (Level 5)	McGinty's Gold (Level 5)	Common Confusions (Levels 3-5)	What is a Sentence? (Levels 3-5)
reading with understanding	▲	▲	▲	○	○	○		
directions and instructions						○		
fact and opinion						▲		
inferences and predictions						▲		
cloze procedure	▲	▲	○	○	▲			
where to look					○	▲		
dictionary work			▲	▲	▲			
telephone directories						○		
timetables						○		
instructions					▲	▲		
maps				▲	▲	○	○	
atlas					▲			
encyclopedia					▲	▲		
reference library				▲	▲	▲		
other sources						▲		

AT3 Writing

	Goblin Winter (Level 2)	Spooky Towers (Level 3)	Spellbound (Level 4)	Pirate's Treasure (Level 4)	Wreckers' Rock (Level 5)	McGinty's Gold (Level 5)	Common Confusions (Levels 3-5)	What is a Sentence? (Levels 3-5)
finishing a sentence		▲						
capital letters/full stops		○						●
making complete sense		○						●
question sentences								●
matching questions/answers					▲			
exclamations								●
mixed-up sentences		▲						
sentence sequencing	▲	▲	▲	▲				
joining sentences						▲		
correcting sentences						▲		
the apostrophe						▲		
direct and indirect speech						▲		
2/3 sentence stories	▲	▲						
3/6 sentence stories	▲	▲						
longer stories	▲	▲	▲	▲	▲	▲		
descriptions				▲	▲	▲		
letters						▲		
"telegram" stories						▲		
headline stories						▲		
recording events					▲	▲		
writing in paragraphs						▲		
verse					▲			
directions and instructions						▲		
writing to suit reader						▲		
explaining processes						▲		
making notes						▲		

ATs1-4 Knowledge about language

	Goblin Winter (Level 2)	Spooky Towers (Level 3)	Spellbound (Level 4)	Pirate's Treasure (Level 4)	Wreckers' Rock (Level 5)	McGinty's Gold (Level 5)	Common Confusions (Levels 3-5)	What is a Sentence? (Levels 3-5)
nouns		▲						
verbs		▲	○					
adjectives		▲						
adverbs						▲		
pronouns						▲		
prepositions		▲						
alphabetical order	▲	▲		▲				
colours	○							
consonants and vowels	○	○						
comparisons	○	▲						
singular and plural	▲	▲						
families	▲							
homes	▲							
occupations	▲							
gender	▲							
groups and collections						▲		
containers				▲				
classification				▲				
sounds			○					
antonyms			○					
synonyms						▲		
homophones								●
rhymes	○	○		▲				
right word in right place	○	○	○	○				
odd man out		▲	○	▲				
word ladders			▲					
word search/recognition			▲	▲	▲			
making words from letters				▲	▲			
word building	○							
correcting spellings		▲						
crosswords			○	○				
anagrams	●	○	○	○				
other word puzzles				▲	○	○		

Cross-curricular

	Goblin Winter (Level 2)	Spooky Towers (Level 3)	Spellbound (Level 4)	Pirate's Treasure (Level 4)	Wreckers' Rock (Level 5)	McGinty's Gold (Level 5)	Common Confusions (Levels 3-5)	What is a Sentence? (Levels 3-5)
Dance	▲							
Art and Craft	▲	▲	▲	▲	▲	▲		
Music	▲							
Cookery	▲							
Topic Work and Projects	▲	▲	▲	▲	▲	▲		

Level 5: Cassette

Side 1

Track	Master	Skill		Tape Counter
1	5.1j	From *The Runaway Summer*: main idea/cause and effect **AT2/5b**		_____
	5.1k	From *The Runaway Summer*: looking for evidence **AT2/5b**		
2	5.1l	listening for detail/recognition of repetition of same idea in different words **AT2/5b**		_____
3	5.2l	From *The Machine Gunners*: recall of detail **AT2/5b**		_____
4	5.2m	comparison of two descriptions of same place points of view/fact and opinion **AT2/5b-c**		_____
5	____	from 'News' by Aiden Chambers & 'The Blind Men and the Elephant' by John Godfrey Saxe: appreciation/points of view/fact and opinion **AT2/5b** There is no activity sheet for this track. It links with page 38 in the pupil's book.		_____
6		'News Room': telephoned news reports, a taped interview and a live commentary		_____
	5.3m	logging the phone calls: selection/main idea **AT3/5a**		
	5.3n	listening for detail/making notes Please see Unit 3 teacher's notes ('News Editor') for ideas on using this material. **AT3/5a**		

Side 2

Track	Master	Skill		Tape Counter
1	5.3u	Chocolate biscuit promotion: following arguments/selecting suitable music for an advertisement **AT2/5a-b; AT3/5c-e**		_____
2	5.4g	From *A Night to Remember*: aural memory with prior instructions to pick out certain details **AT2/5d; AT3/5a-d**		_____
3	5.5b	evaluating a speaker's attitude/points of view **AT2/5b-c**		_____
4	5.5l	evaluating a speaker's attitude/prejudice **AT1/5b; AT2/5b**		_____
5	5.6c	following an argument/persuasion/ pressure/emotionally charged words **AT1/5b; AT2/5b; AT2/5d; AT3/5a-e**		

Answer Cards for Listening Skill Masters

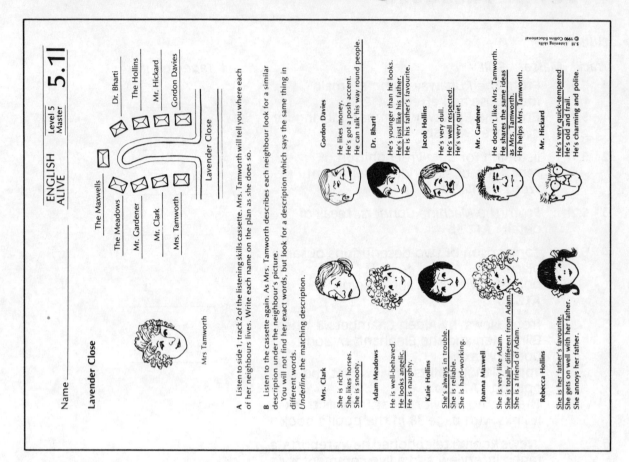

Name

Lavender Close

Mrs Tamworth

The Maxwells
The Meadows
Mr. Gardener
Mr. Clark
Mrs. Tamworth

Dr. Bharti
The Hollins
Mr. Hickard
Gordon Davies

Lavender Close

A Listen to side 1, track 2 of the listening skills cassette. Mrs. Tamworth will tell you where each of her neighbours lives. Write each name on the plan as she does so.

B Listen to the cassette again. As Mrs. Tamworth describes each neighbour look for a similar description under the neighbour's picture. You will not find her exact words, but look for a description which says the same thing in different words.
Underline the matching description.

Mrs. Clark
She is rich.
She likes horses.
She is snooty.

Adam Meadows
He is well-behaved.
He looks angelic.
He is naughty.

Katie Hollins
She's always in trouble.
She is reliable.
She is hard-working.

Joanna Maxwell
She is very like Adam.
She is totally different from Adam.
She is a friend of Adam.

Rebecca Hollins
She is her father's favourite.
She gets on well with her father.
She annoys her father.

Gordon Davies
He likes money.
He's got a posh accent.
He can talk his way round people.

Dr. Bharti
He's younger than he looks.
He's just like his father.
He is his father's favourite.

Jacob Hollins
He's very dull.
He's well respected.
He's very quiet.

Mr. Gardener
He doesn't like Mrs. Tamworth.
He shares the same ideas as Mrs. Tamworth.
He helps Mrs. Tamworth.

Mr. Hickard
He's very quick-tempered.
He's old and frail.
He's charming and polite.

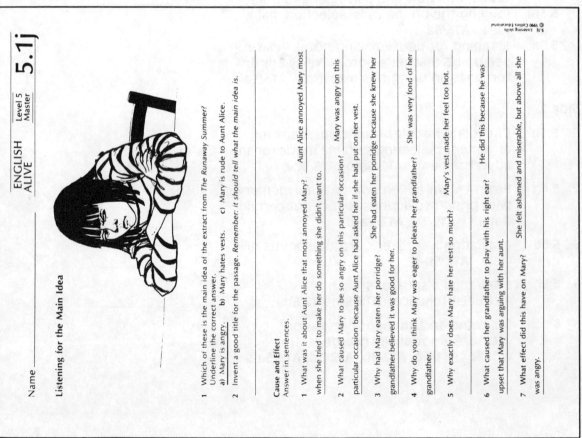

Name

Listening for the Main Idea

1 Which of these is the main idea of the extract from *The Runaway Summer*? Underline the correct answer.
a) Mary is angry. b) Mary hates vests. c) Mary is rude to Aunt Alice.
2 Invent a good title for the passage. *Remember: it should tell what the main idea is.*

Cause and Effect
Answer in sentences.
1 What was it about Aunt Alice that most annoyed Mary? Aunt Alice annoyed Mary most when she tried to make her do something she didn't want to.
2 What caused Mary to be so angry on this particular occasion? Mary was angry on this particular occasion because Aunt Alice had asked her if she had put on her vest.
3 Why had Mary eaten her porridge? She had eaten her porridge because she knew her grandfather believed it was good for her.
4 Why do you think Mary was eager to please her grandfather? She was very fond of her grandfather.
5 Why exactly does Mary hate her vest so much? Mary's vest made her feel too hot.
6 What caused her grandfather to play with his right ear? He did this because he was upset that Mary was arguing with her aunt.
7 What effect did this have on Mary? She felt ashamed and miserable, but above all she was angry.

Name _____

A Holiday in Shoreham

1 What did Jason like and dislike about Shoreham?

The sandy beaches _____ The tide goes out a long way

The Pleasure Palace _____ The Sandcentre is "a bit of a rip-off"

Rides on trams _____

The zoo _____

2 What did Molly like and dislike about Shoreham?

The three piers _____ Noisy amusement arcades and cheap gift shops

The beach _____ The ugly piers

The trams _____ Dirty, polluted sea

Noise and crowds

Expensive and dangerous rides

3 Why do you think their opinions are so different?

_____

_____

_____

Look at these sentences. Were they spoken by Molly or Jason?
Match the sentence to its speaker.

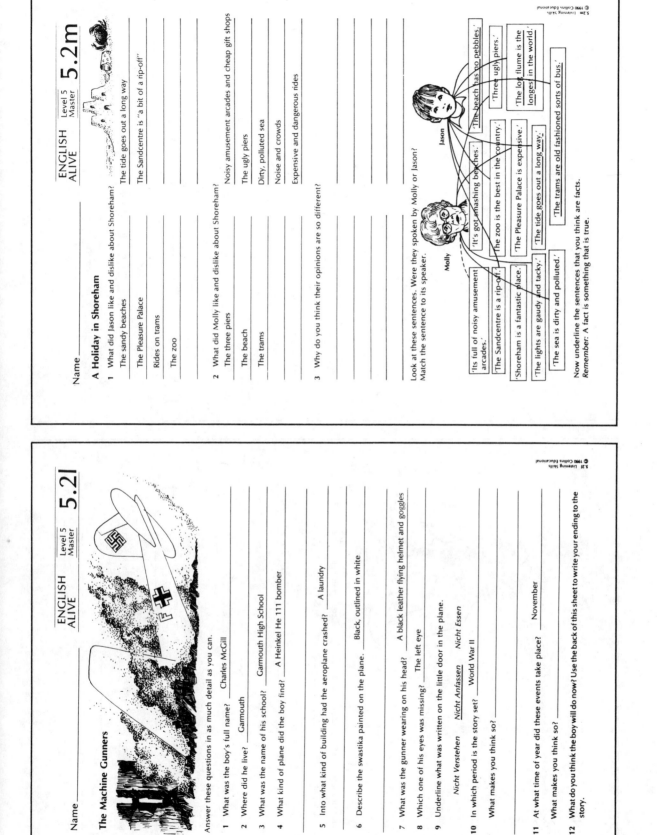

Jason

Molly

'The beach has no pebbles.'

'Three ugly piers.'

'The log flume is the longest in the world.'

'It's got smashing beaches.'

'The zoo is the best in the country.'

'It's full of noisy amusement arcades.'

'The Sandcentre is a rip-off.'

'The Pleasure Palace is expensive.'

'The tide goes out a long way.'

'The trams are old fashioned sorts of bus.'

'Shoreham is a fantastic place.'

'The lights are gaudy and tacky.'

'The sea is dirty and polluted.'

Now underline the sentences that you think are facts.
Remember: A fact is something that is true.

5.2m Listening Skills
© 1990 Collins Educational

Name _____

The Machine Gunners

Answer these questions in as much detail as you can.

1 What was the boy's full name? _____ Charles McGill

2 Where did he live? _____ Garmouth

3 What was the name of his school? _____ Garmouth High School

4 What kind of plane did the boy find? _____ A Heinkel He 111 bomber

5 Into what kind of building had the aeroplane crashed? _____ A laundry

6 Describe the swastika painted on the plane. _____ Black, outlined in white

7 What was the gunner wearing on his head? _____ A black leather flying helmet and goggles

8 Which one of his eyes was missing? _____ The left eye

9 Underline what was written on the little door in the plane.

Nicht Verstehen   Nicht Anfassen   Nicht Essen

10 In which period is the story set? _____ World War II

What makes you think so? _____

11 At what time of year did these events take place? _____ November

What makes you think so? _____

12 What do you think the boy will do now? Use the back of this sheet to write your ending to the story.

5.2l Listening Skills
© 1990 Collins Educational

117

5.3n

ENGLISH ALIVE — Level 5 Master

Name _____

News Room — 2

Use this sheet to make notes for the first two news stories on Level 5 cassette: side 1, track 6.
Answer the questions, but remember that sometimes you are not given sufficient information to answer every question.
Copy the headings on a separate sheet and make notes on the remaining stories.

Bad Smell in Smith Street

Who did it? _____?_____

Where did it happen? _____ Smith St. _____

When did it happen? _____ (Write time of call here) _____

What happened? _____ There is still a bad smell _____

_____

Why did it happen? _____?_____

_____

How did it end? _____?_____

_____

Accident on the M62

Who did it? _____?_____

Where did it happen? _____ Between junctions 6 and 7 on the M62 _____

When did it happen? _____ (Write time of call here) _____

What happened? _____ Sixteen vehicle pile up _____

_____

Why did it happen? _____ Collision between a tanker of hydrochloric acid and an articulated lorry _____

How did it end? _____ Firemen attempting to cut survivors out _____

_____

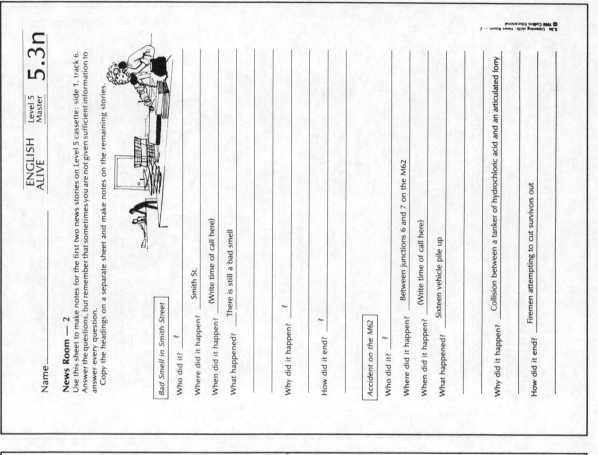

5.3n Listening skills: News Room — 2
© 1990 Collins Educational

5.3m

ENGLISH ALIVE — Level 5 Master

Name _____

News Room — 1

Use this sheet to log the five telephone calls on side 1, track 6 of the Level 5 listening skills cassette.

1

Tape counter number _____

Time to call _____

Name of caller _____ John Dawson _____

Nature of call _____ Bad smell in Smith Street. _____

2

Tape counter number _____

Time to call _____

Name of caller _____ Ken Johnson _____

Nature of call _____ M62 accident _____

3

Tape counter number _____

Time to call _____

Name of caller _____ No name given _____

Nature of call _____ Explosion in Smith St. _____

4

Tape counter number _____

Time to call _____

Name of caller _____ Mr. Hodgson _____

Nature of call _____ Strange creature sighted _____

5

Tape counter number _____

Time to call _____

Name of caller _____ Phil Palmer _____

Nature of call _____ Fire in Smith St. _____

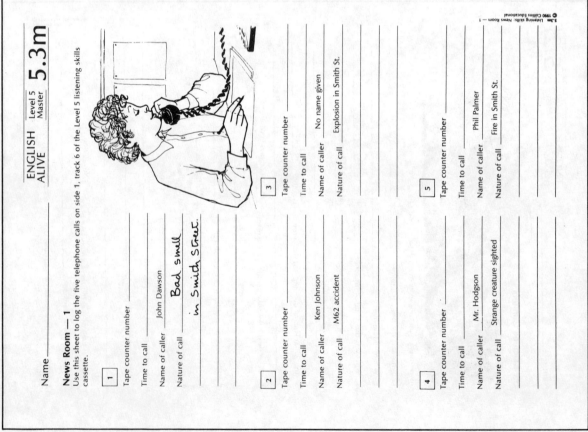

5.3m Listening skills: News Room — 1
© 1990 Collins Educational

ENGLISH ALIVE | Level 5 Master **5.5b**

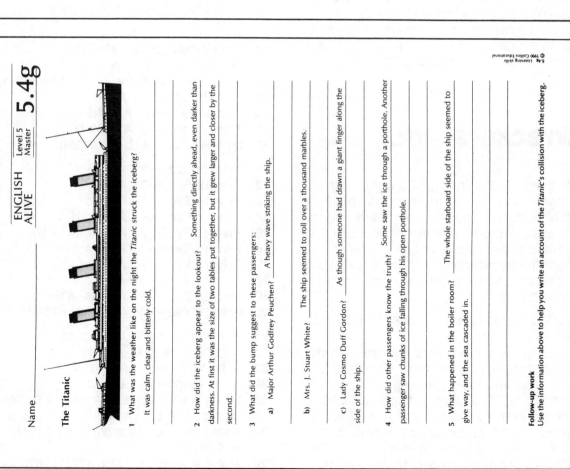

The Chadwick Bypass

1 Is Fred Sedley, the chef of the Carlton Café, in favour of the bypass? ___ He is against the bypass.

2 What reason does he give for this? ___ Less traffic would bring less money into the town.

3 On what point does Councillor Joe Simmonds agree with Fred? ___ Motorised transport made Chadwick prosperous.

4 In what way does he disagree with him? ___ Less traffic would be a good thing for Chadwick.

5 What advantage does he say the bypass might bring? ___ There might well be more shoppers coming into town, because there will be more places to park.

6 Do you think Councillor Simmonds is for or against the bypass? ___ He is for the bypass. Give a reason for your answer. ___ He says shoppers' cars will be a good swop for lorries.

7 What does he hope the result of the inquiry will be? ___ He hopes the inquiry will decide in favour of the bypass

8 Both men refer to the traffic through Chadwick in ways which show how they feel about it. Listen to the cassette again.
  a) Which words does Fred use to show how important he thinks the traffic is to Chadwick? ___ "The life-blood of this town" and "the heartbeat of Chadwick."
  b) Which words tell us Councillor Simmonds' attitude to heavy lorries? ___ "Thundering juggernauts!"

5.5b Listening skills
© 1990 Collins Educational

ENGLISH ALIVE | Level 5 Master **5.4g**

The Titanic

1 What was the weather like on the night the *Titanic* struck the iceberg? ___ It was calm, clear and bitterly cold.

2 How did the iceberg appear to the lookout? ___ Something directly ahead, even darker than darkness. At first it was the size of two tables put together, but it grew larger and closer by the second.

3 What did the bump suggest to these passengers:
  a) Major Arthur Godfrey Peuchen? ___ A heavy wave striking the ship.

  b) Mrs. J. Stuart White? ___ The ship seemed to roll over a thousand marbles.

  c) Lady Cosmo Duff Gordon? ___ As though someone had drawn a giant finger along the side of the ship.

4 How did other passengers know the truth? ___ Some saw the ice through a porthole. Another passenger saw chunks of ice falling through his open porthole.

5 What happened in the boiler room? ___ The whole starboard side of the ship seemed to give way, and the sea cascaded in.

Follow-up work
Use the information above to help you write an account of the *Titanic's* collision with the iceberg.

5.4g Listening skills
© 1990 Collins Educational

Adventures in English

Adventures in English is a series of computer programs for the BBC Micro. Each program comes complete with an accompanying Pressure-fax book of spiritmaster activity sheets which re-inforce the learning objectives. There is an adventure to complement each book of the *English Alive* course.

The adventure programs develop logical thought and problem-solving skills. By creating situations which stretch the pupils' imagination and take them beyond everyday experiences they will provide the stimulus for a wide variety of follow-up work across the curriculum. A chart on page 112 shows the skills targeted for each program.

Wreckers' Rock provides useful follow-up material for Unit 2, while *McGinty's Gold* is the ideal complement to Unit 3.

In addition to these adventures are two further programs available on one disc: *What is a Sentence?* and *Some Common Confusions*. They are ideal remedial aids for teaching essential, basic sentence construction and to distinguish between homophones. These programs do not have an accompanying Pressure-fax book.

Wreckers' Rock

Wreckers' Rock consists of a computer program and a Pressure-fax book of 28 activity sheets. The program encourages the children to use detective work to find out and thwart the plans of a gang of modern-day wreckers. It gives experience in decision-making, problem solving and research skills.

The Pressure-fax book is divided into four sections.

Sheets 1-3 are designed for use with the computer program to record progress. (See program notes below.)

Sheets 4-10 develop further the skills needed in the computer program. They are linked closely to the program adventure, often using the same reference material, although requiring more detailed work.

Sheets 11-20 introduce a new adventure called Private Eye. In this the pupil becomes a private detective tracking down a missing person. The adventure calls for a wide range of reference skills as well as simple problem-solving. English skills such as comprehension, cloze procedure and creative writing are all put to the test.

Sheets 21-27 call on the resources of the classroom and library, especially the dictionary, atlas and encyclopedia. The final sheet (28) gives ideas for connected work such as art and craft, creative writing and individual topic work.

Contents

1 Wreckers' Rock — the program 1   **ATs1-3**
2 Wreckers' Rock — the program 2   **ATs1-3**
3 Wreckers' Rock — the program 3   **ATs1-3**

4 Choosing a Book   **AT2/4d**
5 Telephone Directory — 1   **AT2/4d**
6 Telephone Directory — 2   **AT2/4c & d**
7 Bus Timetable   **AT2/4d**
8 Town Plan — 1   **AT2/4d**
9 Town Plan — 2   **AT3/4a-b**
10 Morse Code   **AT2/4d; AT3/4b**

11 Private Eye — 1   **ATs2-3**
12 Private Eye — 2   **AT2/4d**
13 Private Eye — 3   **AT2/4c**
14 Private Eye — 4   **AT2/4c-d**
15 Private Eye — 5   **AT2/4c; AT3/4b**
16 Private Eye — 6   **ATs2-4**
17 Private Eye — 7   **AT2/4c; AT3/4b**
18 Private Eye — 8   **AT2/4c**
19 Private Eye — 9   **AT2/4c; AT3/4b**
20 Private Eye — 10   **AT2/4d; AT3/4b**

21 Finding Things Out   **AT2/4d**
22 Dictionary Work   **AT2/4d**
23 Atlas Work — 1   **AT2/4d**
24 Atlas Work — 2   **AT2/4d**
25 Using an Encyclopedia — 1   **AT2/4d**
26 Using an Encyclopedia — 2   **AT2/4d**
27 Using an Encyclopedia — 3   **AT2/4d; AT3/4c**
28 Make and Do   **AT1/4d; AT2/4d; AT3/4a-c**

McGinty's Gold

Unit 3 provides the ideal introduction to *McGinty's Gold,* the sixth in the *Adventures in English* series.

McGinty's Gold is an adventure in higher order reading skills. It consists of a computer program and a Pressure-fax book of 28 activity sheets.

The program is in two parts. In Part One the pupil is given the role of a junior reporter on a local newspaper. He uses the newspaper's computer database as background for his first story, which is to report on the auction of the household effects of a notorious armed robber who has recently died in prison. He then finds his way to his assignment using an on-screen map. At the auction he bids for a writing desk. Hidden in a secret drawer is McGinty's notebook, which gives directions on how to find the stolen gold bullion.

In Part Two the reporter follows the instructions in the book. This involves solving simple codes, reasoning from an on-screen gazetteer, and comparing McGinty's instructions to the 'real' world he finds and making decisions accordingly. The climax of his investigations comes when he has to cross a marsh by carefully following McGinty's directions. A successful crossing of the marsh results in finding the gold, the arrest of the only member of the McGinty gang still free, a promotion and a reward from the insurance company.

The activity sheets are divided into three sections.

Sheets 1-5 are designed for use with the computer program to record progress. Sheets 1-3 cover Part One of the program and also provide some follow-up work before Part Two is begun. This allows other groups of children to use Part One before the first group begins the second part. Sheets 4 and 5 are record sheets for Part Two along with more follow-up work directly related to the program.

Sheets 6-24 are based on the many different skills needed by workers on a newspaper, including the skills of reporter, sub-editor, sports writer, feature writer, leader writer and news editor. There are activities based on advertisements, letterwriting and a crossword puzzle. A wide range of English skills is covered.

Sheets 25-28 set assignments. These extend further the skills developed in the program, the earlier activity sheets and the *English Alive* course. They provide situations for the pupil to show how well he has mastered these skills. In the final sheet, guidance is given for the production of a class or school newspaper.

Contents

1 McGinty's Gold — the program — 1 (record sheet) **ATs1-3**
2 McGinty's Gold — the program — 2 (record sheet) **ATs1-3**
3 McGinty's Gold — the program — 3 (record sheet/follow-up work) **ATs1-3; AT3/5a-b**
4 McGinty's Gold — the program — 4 (record sheet) **ATs1-3**
5 McGinty's Gold — the program — 5 (record sheet/follow-up work) **ATs1-3; AT3/5a-e**

6 Reporter — 1 (writing from notes) **AT3/5a-e**
7 Reporter — 2 (writing from a given headline/writing from notes) **AT3/5a-e**
8 Reporter — 3 (writing directions) **AT3/5a**
9 Reporter — 4 (reported speech) **AT3/5b**
10 Reporter — 5 (direct speech/explaining a process) **AT3/5a, b & d**
11 Reporter — 6 (descriptions) **AT3/5a, b & d**
12 Sub-Editor — 1 (making up suitable headlines) **AT3/5a, b & d**
13 Sub-Editor — 2 (correcting errors) **ATs2-3**
14 Sub-Editor — 3 (improving sentences) **ATs2-4**
15 Sub-Editor — 4 (improving sentences) **ATs2-4**
16 Feature Writer — 1 (finding and using reference material) **AT2/5d**
17 Feature Writer — 2 (writing from notes and reference material) **AT3/5a, b & d**
18 Feature Writer — 3 (creative writing using reference material) **AT2/5d; AT3/5a-e**
19 Advertisements — 1 (comprehension/correction) **ATs2-4**
20 Advertisements — 2 (fact/opinion/inferences/prediction) **AT2/5b-c**
21 Letters & Crossword (letter writing/crossword) **AT3/5a; ATs2-4**
22 Sports Writer (writing report from notes and an interview) **AT3/5a-e**

23 News Editor (decisions on news stories) **AT3/5a, b & d**

24 Leader Writer (writing to express views) **AT3/5a, b & d**

25 Assignment — 1 (critic/sports writer/fashion writer/interviews) **AT3/5a-e**

26 Assignment — 2 (use of reference library/making notes/writing) **AT2/5d; AT3/5a, b & d**

27 Assignment — 3 (newspaper cuttings/comparing headlines & reports) **AT2/5a, b, c, e**

28 School Newspaper (suggestions and guidelines) **AT3/5a-e**

Wreckers' Rock and the National Curriculum

The chart below shows how *Wreckers' Rock* integrates with the National Curriculum.
This page may be photocopied and used as a pupil's record sheet. Details may then be transferred to any pupil's profile.

ENGLISH KEY STAGE 2, LEVEL 4									
Attainment Target	Description	*Wreckers' Rock* references							
AT1	4c take part in group activity	1	2	3					
	4d participate in presentation	28							
AT2	4c inference, deduction etc.	6	13	14	15	17	18	19	
	4d finding information	4	5	6	7	8	10	12	
		14	20	21	22	23	24	25	
		26	27	28					
AT3	4a organise writing	9	28						
	4b chronological writing	9	10	15	17	19	20	28	
	4c non-chronological writing	27	28						
ATs1-3	4* various skills	1	2	3					
ATs2-3	4* various skills	11							
ATs2-4	4* various skills	16							

Name _____

Date begun _____

Date completed _____

Comments _____

_____

_____

_____ Teacher _____

McGinty's Gold and the National Curriculum

The chart below shows how *McGinty's Gold* integrates with the National Curriculum.
   This page may be photocopied and used as a pupil's record sheet. Details may then be transferred to any pupil's profile.

ENGLISH KEY STAGE 2, LEVEL 5										
Attainment Target	**Description**		*McGinty's Gold* references							
AT1	5b	contribute to discussion	1	2	3	4	5			
	5c	use language effectively	1	2	3	4	5			
AT2	5a	explain preferences	27							
	5b	developing own views	20	27						
	5c	recognise fact and opinion	20	27						
	5d	use information books	16	18	26	27				
AT3	5a	write in variety of forms	3	5	6	7	8	10	11	
			12	17	18	21	22	23	24	
			25	26	28					
	5b	organise writing	3	5	6	7	9	10	11	
			12	17	18	22	23	24	25	
			26	28						
	5c	use of Standard English	5	6	7	10	11	18	22	
			25	28						
	5d	draft and redraft	5	6	7	12	17	18	22	
			23	24	25	26	28			
	5e	purpose, topic & audience	5	6	7	18	22	25	28	
ATs1-3	5*	various skills	1	2	3	4	5			
ATs2-3	5*	various skills	13							
ATs2-4	5*	various skills	14	15	19	21				

Name _____

Date begun _____

Date completed _____

Comments _____

_____

_____

_____ Teacher _____

Level 5: Index

Suffixes: **a, b, c, d, e** etc. indicate **Activity Masters**
Capital **N** indicates **Teacher's notes**
This index also includes Skillmasters from Levels 1-4

Assessment Masters   ATs2-3
adjectives,   **5.6j**
assignment,   **5.6k**
cloze procedure,   **5.6j**
collaborating towards an agreed end,   **5.6k**
completing sentences,   **5.6h**
cycle diagram,   **5.6j**
diagrams,   **5.6j**
direct speech,   **5.6h**
giving instructions,   **5.6j**
group work,   **5.6k**
inference,   **5.6i**
main idea,   **5.6i**
maps,   **5.6k**
modelling,   **5.6j**
narrative,   **5.6h**
presenting findings,   **5.6k**
problem solving,   **5.6k**
reading for detail,   **5.6i**
reading skills,   **5.6i, 5.6j**
sentences, completing,   **5.6h**
scale, maps,   **5.6k**
speculation,   **5.6i**
writing a brochure,   **5.6k**
writing skills,   **5.6h**

Computer Software Links
Adventures in English, Appendices
McGinty's Gold,   **5.3**
Wreckers' Rock,   **5.2**

Computer Use   ATs1-4
Data handling,
   McGinty's Gold
Simulations:
   McGinty's Gold
   Wreckers' Rock
Teaching Aids:
   Some Common Confusions
   What is a Sentence?
   Word processing,   **5.3N**

Extracts & Poems
Alpha-B75-Earth Visitors' Guide, from, John Cunliffe,   **5.6**
Blind Men and the Elephant, The, John Godfrey Saxe,   **5.3**

Bully Asleep, The, John Walsh,   **5.1**
Calf of the November Moon, Hilary Ruben,   **5.6**
Chambers *Thesaurus,* extract,   **5.5**
Chicago Tribune, 16th April, 1912,   **5.4**
Daily Mirror, 16th April, 1912,   **5.4**
Daily Telegraph,   **5.5**
Diddakoi, The, Rumer Godden,   **5.2**
Discovery of the Titanic, The, Dr. Robert D. Ballard,   **5.4**
Early Times, 27th April, 1988, Juliet Buckley, aged 12,   **5.5**
Fish in a Polluted River, Ian Serrallier,   **5.6**
Horses, The, Edwin Muir,   **5.6**
I've Got an Apple Ready, John Walsh,   **5.1**
Machine Gunners, The, Robert Westall,   **5.2I** side 1 track 3
Mad Meals, Michael Rosen,   **5.5**
My Mate Shofiq, Jan Needle,   **5.1**
News, Aidan Chambers,   **5.3**
News cuttings from *The Advertiser* (Oldham), *Daily Express, Sunday Times, Younger News,*   **5.3,** *Daily Telegraph,*   **5.5**
Night to Remember, A, Walter Lord, side 2 track 3
On The Run, Nina Bawden,   **5.6j**
Rag, a Bone and a Hank of Hair, A, Nicholas Fisk,   **5.6**
Revolting Rhymes, Roald Dahl,   **5.5**
Runaway Summer, The, Nina Bawden, side 1 track 1
Song of the Whale, The, Kit Wright,   **5.6**
Sunday Times, 3rd November, 1987,   **5.4**
This Letter's to Say, Raymond Wilson,   **5.5**
TV Kid, The, Betsy Byars,   **5.3**
Wrestling Princess, The, Judy Corbalis,   **5.5**

Language Games   ATs1-3
Childsplay,   **5.1N**
Everyday Sayings,   **5.5N**
Postcards,   **5.2N**
Quiz Shows,   **5.3N**
Who Is It?,   **5.1N**
Your Own TV Quiz Show,   **5.3N**

Listening Skills   ATs1-3
appreciation, side 1 track 5
auditory/visual interpretation,   **5.1I** side 1 track 2, **5.2N**
aural memory,   **5.2I** side 1 track 3, **5.4g** side 2 track 3
listening games:
   Childsplay,   **5.1N**
   Everyday Sayings,   **5.5N**
   Postcards,   **5.2N**
   Who Is It?,   **5.1N**

musical appreciation, **5.3u** side 2 track 1
selection:
  bias, **5.5l** side 2 track 4
  cause and effect, **5.1j** side 1 track 1
  detail, listening for, **5.1l** side 1 track 2, 3,
    5.3m, **5.3n** side 1 track 6, **5.4g** side 2
    track 3
  detail, recall of, **5.2l** side 1 track 3, **5.4g**
    side 2 track 3
  evaluation, **5.3u** side 2 track 1
  evaluation of speaker's attitude, **5.5b**
    side 2 track 3, **5.5l** side 2 track 4, **5.6c**
    side 2 track 5
  following an argument, **5.2m** side 1
    track 4, **5.3u** side 2 track 1, 73, **5.6c** side 2
    track 5
  main idea, **5.1j** side 1 track 1, **5.3m**, **5.3n**
    side 1 track 6
  making notes, **5.3m**, **5.3n** side 1 track 6
  opinion, **5.2m** side 1 track 4, **5.5b** side 2
    track 3, **5.5l** side 2 track 4
  persuasion, **5.6c** side 2 track 5
  points of view, **5.2m** side 1 track 4, side 1
    track 5, **5.5b** side 2 track 3, **5.5l** side 2
    track 4, **5.5c** side 2 track 5
  prejudice, **5.5l** side 2 track 4
  recognition of same idea in different
    words, **5.5l** side 1 track 2
speculation, **5.2l** side 1 track 3

Memory Skills   AT2
aural memory:
  recall of detail, **5.2l** side 1 track 3, **5.4g**
    side 2 track 3

Reading, Reference and Study Skills   AT2
handling information:
  classification, 36-7, 47, 52
  instructions:
    following instructions, **5.3t**, **5.6a**, **5.6N**
    recipes, **5.3r**, **5.3s**
    sequencing, 18-19, 86
re-organising information:
  diagram, explaining a, 46, **5.6j**, 89
  directions from a street plan, **5.2b**
  flow charts, 88
  holiday booking form, 31 & **5.2f**
  lists, 22-23, **5.2i**, 62, **5.6i**
  modelling:
    cycle diagram, **5.6j**
    flow chart, 88
    graphs, **5.5a**
    hierarchies, **5.3e**
    map details, 20, 21 & **5.2c**
    picture strip, **5.5b**
    story board, 54, **5.3q**
    time line, 18-19, 62, **5.4a**

tree diagrams, 30-1
viewpoint, 38, 64
poem, 84
sequencing:
  events in a prose passage, 7
  flow chart, 88
  time line, 18-19, 62, **5.4a**
sorting facts, **5.2h**, **5.2i**, 62, 86
interpreting information:
ambiguity, 79
appreciation, 10-11, 82-3
audience, awareness of, 44, 47, 52-3, 83,
  5.5N
bias, 38-39, 42-3, **5.3i**, **5.3j**
charts, 31
comparison, 28-29, 46, 52, 53, 64-5, 94-5
evaluation, 2-3, 6, 14, 15, 28-29, 30, 36, 38,
  52, 53, 54, 55, 56, **5.3i**, **5.3j**, **5.3p**, 63, 64, 66,
  72, 73, 83, 87, 88, 95
fact and opinion, 14, 15, 28-29, 38-9, 47,
  5.3i, **5.3j**
group prediction, **5.1a-5.1d**, **5.3a-5.3d**,
  5.5a-5.5d, **5.6a-5.6d**
idioms, 9, 79
imaginative response, 10-11, 18-19, 25,
  46, 48, 50, 72, 73, 83, 87, 92, 93, 95
inference, 2-3, 6, 18-19, 22-23, 28-29, 48,
  50, 52, **5.3i**, **5.3j**, 62, 68, 69, 75, 76, 79, 85, 87,
  90-1, 95
irony, 79
maps, 20-21, 68, 70
opinion poll, 14
persuasion, 15, 28-29
plan, **5.2b**
points of view, 14, 15, 28-29, 38-9, 42-3,
  72-3
prediction, 3, **5.3i**
primary sources:
  observation, 26-27, 88, **5.6N**
  survey, 34-5, 51, **5.5N**
projecting, 2-3, 6, 10-11, 12-13, 62, 63, **5.4N**,
  72, 73
reading for details:
  atlas, **5.2d**, **5.2g**, **5.2N**, 32-3, 67
  brochure, 28-32
  chart, 31
  diagram, 46
  encyclopedia, **5.5c**
  evidence, **5.1k**
  Guinness Book of Records, **5.5d**
  map, 20, 21 & **5.2c**, **5.2d**, 70
  multiple sources:
    letter & timetable, **5.2a**
    passage & map, 20, 21
    passage & poem, 94-5
  newspaper article, 64-5, 66-7, 69, **5.3i**,
    5.3j
  opinion poll, 14

passage, 18-19, 21, **5.2i**, 66-7, **5.6i**, 85, 87, 94

pictures, 93

plan, **5.2b**

poem, 85, 95

reference books, 20, 22, **5.2e, 5.2g, 5.2N**, 32-33, 67, **5.4c, 5.4d, 5.4e, 5.5c**, 85, 91, 92, 93

timetable, railway, **5.2a**

TV programme guide, 47

Venn diagrams, 8

making notes, 54, **5.3p**

reading for the main idea, 36, **5.3k-5.3n**, 62, 84, **5.6i**

reasoning, 26-7, **5.2d, 5.3i, 5.3j**, 70

reference material:

advertisements, 53, 54

atlas, 24, **5.2d, 5.2g, 5.2N**, 32-3, 67

booklets, 32-3

books, 20, 22, **5.2e, 5.2g, 5.2N**, 32-33, **5.1i**, 67, **5.4c, 5.4d, 5.4e, 5.5c**, 85, 91, 92, 93

brochures, 29

encyclopedia, **5.1i, 5.5c**

Guinness Book of Records, **5.5d**

instructions, **5.3t**

newspapers, 36-7, 42-3, **5.3i, 5.3j**, 64-6, 69

opinion poll, 14

plans, **5.2b**

posters, 32-33

recipes, **5.3r, 5.3s**

timetable, **5.2a**

TV programme guide, 47

Venn diagrams, 8

making up own questions, 8, 36-7, 93

speculation, 10-11, 19, 20, 22, **5.2l**, 48, **5.3i, 5.3j**, 63, 64, **5.6i**, 89, 90-1, 93, 95

locating information:

atlas, 24, **5.2d, 5.2g, 5.2N**, 32-33, 67

dictionary:

abbreviations, 75

context clues, 22, 90-1

etymology, 74-5

finding definitions, 74-5, 84

encyclopedia, **5.1i**, 67, 74-5, **5.5c**

finding reasons, 62, 66

Guinness Book of Recods, **5.5d**

library skills:

using reference books, **5.1i, 5.2e, 5.2g, 5.2N**, 67, **5.4c, 5.4d, 5.4e**, 91, 92, 93

search reading, **5.3f**

scanning, 36-7, 64-5

skimming, 36-7, 47

thesaurus, 77

topic sentences, 36-7

reading strategies:

cloze procedure, 49, **5.4b, 5.6j**, 94

context clues, 20, 22, **5.2d**, 48, 74, 84, 90-1

Skillmaster (Level 5)   ATs1-4

comparison of adjectives, **5.1e, 5.1f**

direct and reported speech, **5.3g, 5.3h**

future tense, **5.5g**

letter writing, **5.1g**

search reading, **5.3f**

verbs:

future tense, **5.5g**

past tense with auxiliary verb, **5.2k**

Skillmasters (Complete Index)   ATs1-4

a & an, **1.7a**

abbreviations in speech, **4.2b**

addressing an envelope, **1.3c**

adjectives, **1.5a**

adjectives, comparison of, **3.8c, 5.1e, 5.1f**

adverbs, **3.6a**

adverbs, manner, **2.8b**

alphabet, the, **1.1a**

alphabetical order, 1st letter, **1.1b**

alphabetical order, 2nd letter, **1.13a**

alphabetical order, **3.1a**

alphabetical order of fiction books, **1.14b**

apostrophe:

abbreviation, **3.3b**

possession, **3.3a**

contents list, using a, **4.3b**

context clues, **2.5a**

correcting writing, **4.3f**

date, writing the, **1.11b**

date, writing in numbers, **3.8a**

describing people, **4.1f**

dictionary, arrangement of words, **1.14d**

direct speech, **3.7b**

direct and reported speech, **5.3g, 5.3h**

fiction & non-fiction, **1.14a**

future tense, **5.5g**

his & her, **1.16b**

homonyms, **2.5c**

homophones:

there & their, **1.17a**

two, too & to, **1.17b**

where, were & wear, **1.18b**

write & right, **1.17a**

improving writing, **4.3e**

index, using, **1.20a, 3.6c**

irregular verbs, **4.7b**

is & are, **1.16a**

is & his, **1.16b**

joining three sentences, **4.4e**

letter of complaint, **3.8b**

letter of invitation, **1.11d**

letter writing, **5.1g**

making notes, **3.5e**

months of the year, **1.11a**

nouns, **3.1b**

nouns, common, **1.2a, 1.2b**
nouns, proper, **1.3a**
plurals, *-s* and *-es,* **1.6a**
  -es, **1.18a**
  -ies, **1.29, 1.29a**
  f to *ve* & *-oes, os,* **2.2a**
  -ies & *-s* endings from *-y* words, **2.7b**
prepositions, **3.10e**
pronouns, **2.7a**
punctuation, **3.6b**
reading for detail, **3.4b**
reporting, **4.4f**
search reading, **5.3f**
sentence building:
  joining with *and,* **1.17b**
  joining with *because,* **2.5b**
  joining with *but,* **1.9c**
  joining with *who* or *which,* **2.6b**
  making sense, **2.1a**
  punctuation, **1.27b**
  questions, **1.3b, 2.2b**
sequence in writing a story, **3.7c**
speech in paragraphs, **4.1e**
speech marks, **3.7b**
verbs:
  future tense, **4.7a, 5.5g**
  general, **1.9b, 4.7a**
  past tense, **2.6a, 3.7a, 4.7a**
  past tense with auxiliary verbs, **5.2k**
  revision, **3.4a**
was & were, **1.16a**
writing process, the, **4.3d**

Speaking Skills AT1-2
accent, **5.5N**
collaborating towards agreed ends, 14, 17,
  26-7, **5.2N,** 34-5, 44, 45, 51, 53, 55, 63, 73,
  5.6k, 85, 93, **5.6N**
causal and dependent relationships, 5, 63,
  85, 87, 88, 89
debates, **5.3N,** 73, 93
dealing with problems in the
  imagination, 10, 26-7, **5.2N,** 38, 44, 55, 56,
  73, **5.5N,** 85, 87, 89, 91, 92, 93, **5.6N**
descriptions, **5.2N**
dialect, **5.5N**
drama, **5.1N, 5.2N, 5.3N, 5.5N**
evaluation, 14, 17, 55, 56, 83, **5.5l,** & **5.5N,** 93
explaining processes, 63, 85
group prediction, **5.1a-5.1d, 5.3a-5.3d,**
  5.5a-5.5d, 5.6a-5.6d
group stories, **5.5N**
interviewing, **5.2N,** 34, 35, 51, 56, **5.3N**
justifying behaviour in role, 63
making recordings:
  audio tape, 16, **5.3N, 5.5N,** 93
  video tape, 17, 55, 57, **5.3N,** 93

oral language games:
  Childsplay, **5.1N**
  Everyday sayings, **5.5N**
  Postcards, **5.2N**
  Quiz Shows, **5.3N**
  Who Is It?, **5.1N**
  Your Own Quiz Show, **5.3N**
persuasion, **5.3N, 5.6N**
points of view, **5.2N, 5.3N,** 73, 93
projecting, 6, 10-11, 12-13, 15, **5.1N, 5.2N,**
  63, **5.4N**
reading stories, **5.5N**
reasoning, 4, 5, 10, 13, 26-7, **5.2N,** 55, 63,
  5.5N, 93, **5.6N**
reflecting on feelings, 5, **5.1N**
reporting on past/present
  experiences, 10, 13, **5.1N, 5.3N, 5.6N**
role play, **5.1N, 5.2N,** 63, **5.3N,** 73, **5.6N**
speeches, 73, 93
speculation, 10, 13, **5.4N,** 89, 91, 93, **5.6N**
Standard English, **5.5N**
story making, **5.2N, 5.5N**
taking part in discussions, **5.1N, 5.2N, 5.3N,**
  5.4N, 63, 73, **5.5l,** & **5.5N, 5.6k,** 93 **5.6N**
talking to young children, 83

Themes
Advertising, **5.3**
Change, **5.5**
Conservation, **5.6**
Environment, **5.6**
Journeys, **5.2**
Living Together, **5.1**
Media, The, **5.3**
Newspapers, **5.3**
Personal Relationships, **5.1**
Pollution, **5.6**
Television, **5.3**
Titanic, **5.4**

Thinking Skills ATs1-3
asking questions, 8, 34, 35, 36-7, 51, **5.3N,**
  62, 63, 93
cloze procedure, 49, **5.4b, 5.6j,** 94
comparison, 46, 52, 53, 64-5, **5.4N,** 94
context clues, 20, 22, **5.2d,** 48, 74, 84, 90-1
dealing with problems in the
  imagination, 10, 26-7, **5.2N,** 38, 44, 55, 56,
  73, **5.5N, 5.6k,** 85, 87, 88, 89, 91, 92, 93, **5.6N**
developing strategies, 22-7
evaluation, 2-3, 6, 14, 15, 17, 28-9, 30, 36, 38,
  52, 53, 54, 55, 56, **5.3p,** 63, 64, 66, **5.3u** side 2
  track 1, 83, **5.5b** side 2 track 3, **5.5l** side 2
  track 4 & **5.5N,** 87, 88, 93
explaining processes, 63, **5.6j,** 86-7
fact and opinion, 14, 15, 28-9, **5.2m,** 38-9,
  47, **5.3i, 5.3j, 5.5b** side 2 track 3, **5.5l** side 2
  track 4 & **5.5N**

group prediction, **5.1a-5.1d, 5.3a-5.3d, 5.5a-5.5d, 5.6a-5.6d**

imaginative response, 10-11, 18-19, 25, 46, 48, 50, 72, 73, 83, 87, 92, 93, 94-5

inference, 2-3, 6, 18-19, 22-3, 48, 50, 52, **5.3i, 5.3j,** 62, 68, 69, 75, 76, 79, 84, **5.6i,** 85, 87, 90-1, 95

persuasion, 15, 28-9, 53, 54, 55, **5.3N, 5.6c** side 2 track 5, **5.6N**

planning:
  advertisements, 53, 55, 56-7, **5.3u** side 2 track 1
  audio tape, **5.3N, 5.5N**
  books, 21, 32-3, 83
  conducting an experiment, 26-7, 88
  inquiry into the *Titanic* disaster, 63
  inquiry, public, 73
  interviews, **5.2N,** 34, 35, 51, 56, **5.3N**
  leisure park, **5.6k**
  model making, 70
  newspaper, 44, 45, **5.3k-5.3n**
  newspaper article, 39, 43, 64
  newspaper survey, 34, 35
  opinion poll, 14, **5.3N**
  public inquiry, 73
  snack biscuit to sell, 56-7, **5.3r-5.3u**
  talk, 73
  TV discussion programme, 93
  TV quiz show, **5.3N**
  TV survey, 51
  video tape, 17, 32-3- 55, 57, **5.3N,** 93

points of view, 14, 15, 28-9, **5.2m, 5.2N,** 38-9, 42-3, 72-3, **5.6c** side 2 track 5, 93

problem solving, 10, 26-7, **5.2N,** 34, 35, 38, 44, 45, 51, 55, 56-7, **5.3N, 5.3o,** 68, **5.6k,** 85, 87, 88, 89, 91, 92, **5.6N**

projecting, 2-3, 6, 10-11, 12-13, 15, **5.1N, 5.2N,** 62, 63, **5.4N,** 72, 73, **5.6N**

reasoning, 4, 5, 10, 13, 26-7, **5.2N,** 55, **5.3i, 5.3j,** 63, 70, 85, **5.6k,** 93, **5.6N**

re-organising information:
  flow charts, 88
  lists, 22, 62, **5.6i**
  modelling:
    cycle diagram, **5.6j**
    diagrams, **5.6j**
    flow chart, 88
    graphs, **5.5a**
    hierarchies, **5.3e**
    map details, 20, 21 & **5.2c**
    picture strips, **5.6b**
    story board, 54, **5.3q**
    time line, 18-19, 62, **5.4a**
    tree diagrams, 30-31
    Venn diagrams, 8
    viewpoint, 38, 64, 93
  newspaper report based on passage, 64

sequencing, 7, 18-19, 62, **5.4a,** 86

sorting, **5.2h, 5.2i,** 62, 86

speculation, 3, 10-11, 13, 19, 22, **5.2l,** 48, **5.3i, 5.3j,** 63, 64, **5.4N, 5.6i,** 89, 90-1, 93, 95, **5.6N**

Word Study   ATs1-4
acronyms, 74-5
adjectives, **5.6j**
adjectives, comparison, **5.1e, 5.1f**
ambiguity, 79
Americanisms, **5.5e**
antonyms, 80
colloquial expressions, 9, **5.5N**
compound words, 5, **5.1h,** 74
definitions, 4, **5.1N,** 74-5
double negatives, 79
etymology, 74-5
figurative language, 9, **5.5N**
idioms, 9, **5.1N,** 79, **5.5N**
irony, 79
malapropisms, 79
matching place names to meanings, 68
metaphor, 25
national names, 24
new words:
  acronyms, 74-5
  borrowing from other languages, 74-5
  compound words, 74-5
  from names, 74-5
  from other languages, 74-5
  from science, 74-5
  old words with new meanings, 74-5
  slang, 74-5
palindromes, 75
place name origins, 22-3, 68
prefixes, 5, **5.2k,** 80, **5.5f**
pronunciation, **5.5N**
rhymes, 25
root words, 5
shades of meaning, 22-3
similes, 25
slang, 74-5
spelling, 77, **5.5N**
spoonerisms, 79
suffixes, 5
synonyms, 77
thesaurus, 77
verb tense, 81, **5.5g**
word search, **5.4f**
words from other languages, 22-3

Writing Skills   AT3
The writing process:
asking questions, 18, 36-7
antonyms, 80
direct speech, 40-41, **5.3N,** 80, **5.6h**
ellipsis, 80
improving writing, 45
making own books, 83, **5.6k**

plot, **5.5N**
reported speech, 80
reporting, 38-9, 43, 44, 45
rhyming schemes, 25
speech:
   direct speech, 40-1, **5.3N**, 80, **5.6h**
   play dialogue, 13, 55
   reported speech, 40-1, **5.3N**, 80
spelling, checking, 77
synonyms, 80
titles, headlines, 36-7, **5.6i**
thoughts and feelings, 51
variety in sentences, **5.6h**
Forms and styles of writing:
writing for different audiences, 13, 16, 17,
   28-9, **5.2N**, 34, 39, 44, 45, 49, 50, 51, 53, 54, 55,
   72, 73, 83, **5.5N**, 85, 95, **5.6N**
expressive:
   autobiography, **5.1N**
   imaginative writing as participant, 5, 48
poetic:
   books for younger children, 83
   descriptive prose, 21, 28-9, 48, 70, 93
   dialogue for acting, 55, **5.5N**
   essay, 73
   expressing thoughts around a
      subject, 49, 50, **5.3u** side 2 track 1, 73
   found poems, 78
   images, 25
   imaginative story, 11, 26-7, 83
   list poem, 4, 78
   limericks, 25
   menu, amusing, 78
   metaphor poem, 25
   newspaper stories from headlines, 39
   plays, 13, 55, **5.5N**
   plot, **5.5N**
   poems from inkblot patterns, **5.1N**
   poems from photographs, 25
   postcard, 30
   recipe, amusing, 78
   re-telling stories, **5.5N**
   simile poem, 25
   spoonerisms, 78
   story starters, 83, 91
   'tree' poem, 89
   verse:
      about an endangered species, 92
      found poems, 78
      from inkblot patterns, **5.1N**
      from newspaper articles, **5.3N**
      from photographs, 25
      list poems, 4, 78
      metaphor, 25
      nursery rhymes with a twist, 82
      plan for writing, 82
      simile poem, 25
      'tree' poem, 89

   using a model, 4, 78, 82, 89
transactional:
advertisements, 32-3, 53, 54-5, 56-7, **5.3o**,
   5.3u side 2 track 1
instructions:
   explaining how to do something, 26-7,
      86-7, 88, 96
   explaining how to make
      something, 26-7, **5.6j**
   explaining how something works, 46
letters:
   asking for information, **5.2N**
   audio cassette, 16
   complaint, 28-9
   expressing opinions, 17, 49, **5.3N**
   protest, 72, 73
   reply to invitation, **5.2a**, 85
   setting out:
      envelope, 17
      letter, **5.1g**
   to a newspaper, **5.3N**
   to a pen pal, 16
   to a television station, 49
recording explicit contents of passage,
   etc.:
   advertisement, evaluation of, 54, **5.3p**
   details, 18-19, 84
   drawing a picture, 28-9
   explaining processes from a
      diagram, 46, 89
   flow diagram, 88
   from different view points, 15, **5.1N**, 38,
      43, 44, 62, 64, **5.5N**
   giving directions, 20, **5.2b**
   main ideas, 2, 84
   making lists, **5.2i**, 62
   maps, putting details on, 21 & **5.2c**
   picture strips, **5.6b**
   same idea in different words, 9, 84
   sequencing, 7, 19, 62, 86
   sorting facts, **5.2h**, **5.2i**, 62, 86
   time line, 19, 62
   tree diagram, 30-1
recording information:
   audio cassette, 16, 93
   advertisement, 53, 54, 55, 56-7, **5.3o**, **5.3u**

   changes in a local district recorded as a
      book, 72
   chart, **5.3e**, 86-7, 88
   board game, 96
   book review, **5.3N**
   brochure, 32-3, **5.6k**
   cycle diagram, **5.6j**
   designing packaging, 56-7, **5.3o**, **5.3t**
   diagrams, 8, **5.6j**
   explaining processes, 46, 86-7, 88
   flow chart, 88

guide books, 32-3
graphs, **5.5a**
holiday booking form, 30-1 & **5.2f**
instructions for board game, 96
leaflets, 73
lists, 49, 62
main ideas of a newspaper report, 36,
  5.3k-5.3n
main ideas of captioned pictures, 46
magazine, **5.3N**
map, 3D model, 70
maps, **5.6k**
menu, 78
newspaper, 44-5, **5.3N**
news stories, 36-7, 38-9, 43, 44, 45, **5.4N**
newspaper headlines and report, 39, 64
notes, making, 39, **5.3n**, 73, 85, 87, 89, 91
opinion poll, 14
passport, 32-3
photographs, 72
phrase book, **5.2N**
picture strips, **5.6b**
planning a world tour, 32-3, **5.2N**
poster, **5.2N**, 56-7, 73, 89
recipe, 56-7, **5.3r-5.3s**, 78
reviews, 49, **5.3N**
solutions to problems, 26-7
story board, 54-5, **5.3q**
telephone conversation, **5.3m, 5.3n**
time line, 19, 62
tree diagram, 30-1
use of reference material,
  audio tape, **5.3u**
  books, **5.2e,** 85, 91, 92
  video tape, 54
Venn diagrams, 8, **5.1N**
video tape, 17, 32-3, 55, 56-7, 93

National Curriculum of England and Wales: English Level 5

Attainment target 1: speaking and listening

a   Give a well organised and sustained account of an event, a personal experience or an activity.

b   Contribute to and respond constructively in discussion, including the development of ideas; advocate and justify a point of view.

c   Use language to convey information and ideas effectively in a straightforward situation.

d   Contribute to the planning of, and participate in, a group presentation.

e   Recognise variations in vocabulary between different regional or social groups, and relate this knowledge where appropriate to personal experience.

Attainment target 2: reading

a   Demonstrate, in talking and writing about a range of stories and poems which they have read, an ability to explain preferences.

b   Demonstrate, in talking or writing about fiction, poetry, non-fiction and other texts that they are developing their own views and can support them by reference to some details in the text.

c   Show in discussion that they can recognise whether subject matter is non-literary and media texts is presented as fact or opinion.

d   Select reference books and other information materials and use organisational devices to find answers to their own questions and those of others.

e   Show through discussion an awareness of a writer's choice of particular words and phrases and the effect on the reader.

Attainment target 3: writing

a   Write in a variety of forms for a range of purposes and audiences, in ways which attempt to engage the interest of the reader.

b   Produce, independently, pieces of writing in which the meaning is made clear to the reader and in which organisational devices and sentence punctuation, including commas and the setting out of direct speech, are generally accurately used.

c   Demonstrate increased effectiveness in the use of Standard English (except in contexts where non-standard forms are needed for literary purposes) and show an increased differentiation between speech and writing.

d   Assemble ideas on paper or on a VDU, individually or in discussion with others, and show evidence of an ability to produce a draft from them and then to revise and redraft as necessary.

e   Show in discussion the ability to recognise variations in vocabulary according to purpose, topic and audience and whether language is spoken or written, and use them appropriately in their writing.

Attainment target 4/5: presentation

Pupils should be able to:

a   Spell correctly, in the course of their own writing, words of greater complexity.

b   Check final drafts of writing for misspelling and other errors of presentation.

c   Produce clear and legible handwriting in printed and cursive styles.